Institute of Classical Architecture & Art
20 West 44th Street, Suite 310, New York, NY 10036
Telephone: (212) 730-9646 Facsimile: (212) 730-9649
www.classicist.org

Peter Lyden, President
Classicist Committee of the ICAA Board of Directors:
Anne Kriken Mann and Gary Brewer, Co-Chairs;
Alexa Hampton, Michael Mesko, David Rau, David Rinehart, Suzanne Santry

Guest Editor: Charles D. Warren
Managing Editor: Stephanie Salomon

ACKNOWLEDGMENTS

The ICAA gratefully acknowledges the Gladys Krieble Delmas Foundation for its generous support of *Classicist* No. 14.

The ICAA, *Classicist* Committee, and guest editor of *Classicist* No. 14 wish to recognize the extraordinary contribution of Andrew Prokos for the cover photography and Anne Day for images throughout *Classicist* No.14, and we extend our gratitude to TF Cornerstone for making available its rooftop for the cover photograph. We thank all the members of the ICAA staff who contributed their efforts, particularly Mimi Bradley for her steadfast support in making *Classicist* 14 a reality. We are grateful to the anonymous peer reviewers for their diligence and insight, the staff of Avery Architectural and Fine Arts Library for its unfailing assistance, and Erica Stoller for help with illustrations. The generosity of numerous collaborators who submitted work, offered advice, and contributed material to *Classicist* No. 14 is greatly appreciated.

MISSION STATEMENT

The *Classicist* is an annual peer-reviewed journal dedicated to the advancement of the core values of the Institute of Classical Architecture & Art by providing a venue for scholarship, a forum for current classical practice, and a source of information and inspiration for students, practitioners, teachers, patrons, and lovers of classical art and architecture.

PHOTO CREDITS

Front & back covers: lower Manhattan, photographed exclusively for the *Classicist*.
© Andrew Prokos—www.andrewprokos.com

Front endpapers: New York and Brooklyn, Currier & Ives, ca. 1875. Source: Geography and Map Division, Library of Congress, Washington, D.C.

Page 63: Grand Central Terminal. Photo: © Anne Day.

Page 81: The old Police Building cupola on Centre Street in Manhattan. Photo: Chuck Pefley/Alamy Stock Photo.

Page 97: Standard Oil Building, 26 Broadway at Bowling Green in lower Manhattan, New York. Photo: Kenneth Grant/NewYorkitecture.com.

Back endpapers: Aerial view of midtown Manhattan, New York, looking downtown, toward the Rockefeller Center and the Empire State Building, ca. 1955. Photo: Hulton Archive/Getty Images.

Design: Suzanne Ketchoyian, Rauffenbart Partners, Inc.
Printing: Allied Printing Services, Manchester, CT

CLASSICIST № 14

NEW YORK CITY

FOREWORD

I became an architect because I loved the buildings of my city, New York, and imagined one day that I would make ones like them—
not the same ones, but ones that like them were imbued with the spirit of confidence and dignity ... The New York of my youth is to this day
the principal subject of all my work in architecture.—Robert A.M. Stern, *Toward a Modern Architecture After Modernism,* 1981.

New York is my city. I live here. I work here. The screeching subway trains, the low-lying sprawl of the outer boroughs' hundred-year-old suburbia, the shimmering towers that rise above the bay to form Manhattan's skyline—all are part of a scene that continues to thrill and inspire me. Of all the places that I love, I am most proud, as an architect, of this city.

When I was growing up, from my childhood home in Brooklyn, the skyscrapers of Manhattan seemed part of an Emerald City, my personal Oz, a great movie set through which I could wander freely. And as I came to wander more purposefully, I came to appreciate what the critic Montgomery Schuyler called the gallery of New York's streets, referring in particular to Manhattan's blocks of townhouses, each varied, each indebted to precedent, which made a stroll down city streets so like walking through a museum. In my college days, Adolf Placzek, librarian at Columbia's Avery Library, brought I. N. Phelps Stokes's amazing *Iconography of Manhattan Island* to my attention, deepening my understanding of how the magical city I loved had come to be.

New York was a center of the great Classical Revival in the late nineteenth and early twentieth centuries. That period saw the expansion of traditional principles of architecture and urbanism across the rapidly growing city's street grid (itself a descendant of the classical Roman town plan) and its adaptation to new types, including the skyscrapers that came to symbolize the city's ascendance as a world capital of finance and culture. Architects of the day—some but not all classically trained—were not seeking to rebuild Rome, but rather to adapt Roman forms to a new world and a new era. The best buildings of my favorite period, the late 1920s and early 1930s—One Wall Street, 40 Wall Street, the Empire State Building—were altogether new, and yet modeled on classical principles. The zoning of the time, which required bringing buildings to the sidewalk up to a certain height before they broke free to reach for the sky, locked the towers into

the urban matrix, ensuring that New York's intensely eclectic streetscapes, with buildings of varying heights and uses jumbled together, shared an attitude toward scale and proportion, relief and materiality, and thereby remained coherent.

During the Great Depression, when commissions for architects were few and far between, classicism atrophied in New York; and by the time construction rebounded in the postwar years the onslaught of International Modernism held sway, overwhelming Manhattan's romantic skyline with bland, inarticulate buildings drained of quality and aspiration; to me they seemed like the empty boxes the earlier skyscrapers might have come in. Yet even in their multitude, these modernist intrusions did not succeed in swamping the vital creative flowering that had preceded them; from sidewalk to skyline, New York remains a city organized on classical principles.

So where are we today? Although a capital "M" Modernist—and in my view too often anti-urban— approach continues to dominate large-scale development in New York, we have enjoyed in parallel a resurgence of interest in the classical approach, and my firm and others represented in this volume have been given opportunities to design important projects that illustrate the enduring power of classical principles to support and celebrate twenty-first-century life. Those that have been realized have met with resounding public acceptance. Yet there is more to be done.

I see myself as an ambassador representing the past to the future. For me, the accumulated experience that we call tradition is fundamental. To embrace tradition is to release architecture from circumstantial action into realms of meaning rooted in the evolving order of the manmade world. New York in its Classical Revival heyday looked to history, and to the classical tradition, for inspiration. Today, that legacy remains for us to explore and study. It offers us important lessons in how to adapt classical principles to new modes of construction and new ways of life. The streets of New York are a history book open before us; if we walk them together, I'm confident they will help us find our way forward.

—Robert A.M. Stern

View from 15 Central Park West, designed by Robert A.M. Stern Architects.

LETTER FROM THE EDITOR

The influence of antiquity on the architecture of New York City can be seen somewhere on almost every block, and many of the city's most beloved places are suffused with the classical tradition. Yet the vast scale of the city and its complex infrastructure combine with skyscrapers and other architectural innovations to make it the quintessential modern metropolis. The encounter between ancient traditions and new technology characterizes the often eclectic cityscape where classical architecture is sometimes pure, but more often a fragment, or a reference to an incompletely realized ideal. As it is everywhere, classical architecture is an unfinished project in New York City, which is the focus of this issue of the *Classicist.*

The antiquarian impulse that is a part of the classical tradition is tempered here by the city's modern situation. Remnants of the colonial past are rare and scattered; much of what was not destroyed by the devastating fires in 1776 and 1835 has been lost to later development. By the early twentieth century, the skyline, once defined by church steeples, had been transformed by bridges of unprecedented span and commercial towers of staggering height. On the ground, the relentlessness of the uptown grid made the spiderweb of narrow streets in lower Manhattan, once central to the city, into an exceptional episode at its edge. This tumult of change and constant construction has led to the city's hybrid architecture and distinctive urbanism where the adjacency of the new and old produces shifts in scale that can be as thrilling as they are tragic.

In this issue of the *Classicist* we explore some encounters between the modern city and the classical tradition. Allan Greenberg's essay addresses New York's most characteristic building type—the skyscraper. Greenberg discusses traditions of style and configuration in New York's tall buildings and how contemporary architects have strayed from the suave urbanism of the celebrated examples we still enjoy. Mark Hewitt's essay describes the relationship between city and country houses which, as Hewitt observes, is not all that different from Renaissance or even Roman patterns. Jon Ritter writes about the triumphal arch in New York and the way it has been used to structure and lend meaning to the plan of the modern city. My own essay considers the steel-frame book stacks at the functional and conceptual heart of one of the city's most elaborately embellished Beaux-Arts–style buildings—the New York Public Library. These essays all touch on the period between the American centennial and the Great Depression, when the integration of modern developments in architecture and classical form enjoyed something of a golden age. To leaven this mix we have included the musing of Stephen Alesch and Robin Standefer on contemporary New York, and a selection of drawings from Columbia University's Avery Architectural & Fine Arts Library, introduced by Janet Parks, the curator who has devoted a long career to caring for and building this renowned collection.

It has been a great pleasure working with these authors, as it has been working with the fine ICAA staff. The Institute's active Classicist Committee has selected and organized the content of the journal's portfolio sections devoted to professional practice and student work. These pages illustrate the vitality of the classical tradition in New York today and the impressive range of classical work being produced by students of architecture and art in the United States and abroad.

—Charles D. Warren
Guest Editor

View of the west facade of the New York Public Library.

TO·THE·GLORY·OF·THE·AMERICAN·NAVY
AND·IN·GREETING·TO·OUR·ADMIRAL
A·GRATEFUL·CITY·RELYING·ON·THEIR·VALOR
HAS·BUILT·THIS·ARCH·MDCCCXCIX

FRAMING THE CITY
NEW YORK'S CITY BEAUTIFUL ARCHES, 1889–1919

JON RITTER

ew York is known as a center of American Renaissance architecture but not as a locus of that movement's analogue in urbanism, the City Beautiful, which promoted prominent sites for monumental buildings.[1] Nevertheless, a City Beautiful conception of coordinated spatial order can be discerned in the relationship between the classically inspired triumphal arches built from 1889 to 1919 and the city's urban fabric. By framing streets and buildings with sculptural arches, architects, politicians, and civic groups proposed an implicit plan, promoting structure for a city that lacked systems of spatial hierarchy and contributing to the emergence of city planning as a profession in the following decades. Before the establishment of zoning regulations and broad municipal regulatory powers in the teens, arches suggested the presence of a civic system regulating urban form through monumentality.

City Beautiful advocates sought to unify and aggrandize American cities with formally planned avenues, parks, and building ensembles inspired by classical antiquity and European Baroque planning. Around 1900, architects, politicians, and civic reform groups proposed to retrofit the gridiron with diagonal avenues terminated by sites for public buildings and institutions, as in the plans proposed by the Municipal Art Society (MAS, 1902), and the New York City Improvement Commission (NYCIC, 1907) (fig. 2).[2] The emphasis on street and circulation systems in these plans highlights a pragmatic aspect of planning that is obscured by the aesthetic emphasis of the term "City Beautiful." Indeed, the movement's advocates sought to reshape both the image and the function of cities by combining

street and infrastructure systems with opportunities for civic embellishment. In Daniel Burnham's later plans for San Francisco and Chicago, for example, street systems radiate from monumental civic centers, focusing on key institutional nodes. Like Burnham, reformers in New York sought to install what Lewis

> By framing streets and buildings with sculptural arches, architects, politicians, and civic groups proposed an implicit plan ...

Mumford identified as the "positional magnificence" of European Baroque planning.[3] Both Baroque planners and City Beautiful advocates sought or devised sites for buildings at axial intersections, to lend visibility, monumentality, and context within the overall urban structure. Rebuilding American cities in this way proved infeasibly expensive, however, and only Philadelphia was able to realize a complete diagonal avenue focused on monumental public buildings.[4]

Given the failure to implement new street plans in New York, architects, politicians, and civic groups turned to triumphal arches to create axial foci and to suggest the potential for coordinated planning in the classical mode. Freestanding ceremonial arches have endured as effective urban objects since the Roman Republic.[5] European neoclassical arches of the eighteenth and nineteenth centuries revived Roman forms to memorialize triumphs and to mark the emergence of new imperial states. In New York, arch builders appropriated the Roman type for similar purposes, insinuating monumental planning into cities without the cost and negotiation of remapping street systems and revising property lines.

Fig. 1. Dewey Arch by Charles R. Lamb and the National Sculpture Society, photographed ca. 1900.

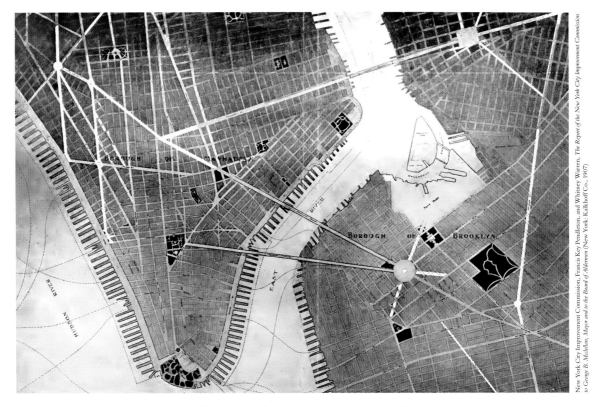

Fig. 2. Detail map of Brooklyn and lower Manhattan by the New York City Improvement Commission, 1907, showing new diagonal streets across gridirons, part of a proposal to integrate infrastructure with civic monuments.

Washington Memorial Arch

Stanford White's permanent arch for Washington Square set the Roman classical precedent for ceremonial and triumphal arches in New York (fig. 3).[6] The location at the terminus of Fifth Avenue exemplifies the power of arches to frame the city through physical and visual relationships to streets and surroundings. City Beautiful leader Charles Mulford Robinson observed that arches like White's created "pomp and majesty … to magnify a city's splendor" by emphasizing urban street axes.[7] The Washington Memorial Arch enjoys positional magnificence, creating a classicizing focus and self-image for the neighborhood, while also defining the urban axis of Fifth Avenue.

Local patrons who sponsored the Washington Arch anticipated that it would influence its surroundings beyond channeling traffic, to assert national identity with classical symbolism. For example, financier Henry G. Marquand argued that the presence of the arch would protect the area from deteriorating into a tenement district. At the 1895 dedica-

tion ceremony, Marquand noted that "[s]ince every high-class work of beauty adds to the attraction and enhances the value of property, we may feel sure that our men of wealth will encourage the building of other arches and public works, that our school of architecture and sculpture will rank high among the modern nations of the earth."[8] Marquand's confidence in the catalyzing effects of the arch helped introduce the concept of coordinated planning during the City Beautiful era. His concerns clearly anticipate the aims of city planners to shape land use in the next generation through legal and technical controls like zoning and municipal regulation.

The Washington Arch also shapes the park landscape, as did the arched bridges of Central Park, which framed views and directed movement along the picturesque pathways of the previous generation. Significantly, Olmsted & Vaux's arched bridges also integrate with infrastructure, forming the layered circulation system the firm innovated in Central Park.[9] White's arch announced a shift to the classical mode, but like the arches of Central

Park, it asserted its urbanism through the relationship to streets and circulation systems. John H. Duncan's Soldiers' and Sailors' Memorial Arch at Grand Army Plaza in Brooklyn similarly marks entry to the park while mediating between the picturesque park landscape and the axial parkway system Olmsted & Vaux developed with Eastern and Ocean Parkways radiating from the plaza (fig. 4).[10]

Dewey Arch

In 1899, the city celebrated Admiral George Dewey's victory over Spain in Manila Bay with the classically inspired Dewey Arch, erected near Madison Square at Twenty-fourth Street (see fig. 1).[11] The site created positional magnificence at the intersection of Fifth Avenue, Twenty-third Street, and Broadway, recalling the axial street systems of Renaissance and Baroque Rome or European Baroque palaces such as Versailles. Like the Washington Arch before it, the Dewey Arch created visual and physical focus on an architectural object placed in contrast with the city's gridiron blocks.

For Robinson, the Dewey Arch implied ramifications beyond temporary celebrations and axial relationships, suggesting a growing civic identity. Noting the organizers' appeal to coordinate the decorations of housefronts along Fifth Avenue, and the cooperation among house owners for later Dewey celebrations in Boston and New Haven, Robinson concluded,

> The importance of cooperation has been observed, to the end that in the decoration of a city there shall be adopted a civic unit—which is to say a street or a block—and not the false or irrelevant unit of the individual. There has

Fig. 3. Washington Memorial Arch, McKim, Mead & White, 1889–92, looking north up Fifth Avenue.

appeared the artistic necessity of harmony and even of evidence of a substantial unanimity—philosophically justified by the thought that the display is one united people's expression of a common feeling. This has been the motive, indeed, for cooperation.[12]

This sense of collective identity set in contrast to individualism indeed motivated City Beautiful reform, from its genesis in the White City of the 1893 World's Columbian Exposition in Chicago to the urban plans of MAS and NYCIC.[13] The unification of American Renaissance architecture with City Beautiful urbanism proposed a public focus for American cities, here anchored around a triumphal arch organizing visual and physical space. Reformers like Robinson understood that temporary arches precipitated comprehensive planning, and they supported the development of legal controls and regulations to implement the collective design suggested by temporary manifestations.[14]

Attention to the context of the Dewey Arch in daily life reminds us of the City Beautiful's limits. Images typically depict it as a dominant urban object directing the axes of the city. A photograph taken three blocks north of Madison Square suggests a different role for the Dewey Arch, however (fig. 5). In this private photograph from a family album, the arch appears subordinate to the uncoordinated irregularity of Fifth Avenue buildings. From this perspective, the arch seems small and unremarkable within the array of traffic, signs, and buildings of diverse sizes, types, and styles. This image recalls exactly what the City Beautiful sought to reform

11

Fig. 4. Grand Army Plaza, Brooklyn in 1938. McKim, Mead & White incorporated John H. Duncan's arch (center) into the design of the plaza to define this space as the focal point of Olmsted & Vaux's parkways.

Fig. 5. Dewey Arch by Charles R. Lamb, looking north from 21st Street. The arch remained standing for over a year.

in the urban landscape—the chaotic, unplanned urban fabric of the improvised and individualistic city.[15] The weak influence of the Dewey Arch on its neighborhood suggests the failure of the City Beautiful to replan New York, as well as the perseverance of individualism over Robinson's collective urban ideal.

Efforts to rebuild the Dewey Arch as a permanent fixture failed after Dewey entered national politics,[16] but even its temporary presence contributed to the concept of urban planning. The arch crystalized Robinson's vision of social cooperation and Marquand's aspiration to influence neighborhood development. Later planners would take up these same concepts, but they would locate them in the regulatory legal systems of what came to be called the City Practical or the City Scientific.[17] More broadly, the Dewey Arch implied planning as spatial coordination, as proposed in the later MAS and NYCIC plans. Positional magnificence suggested a plan at work in the city, connecting key sites and nodes rather than isolating them on gridiron blocks. In the era before the establishment of city plan-

ning as a technical and legal discipline, arches represented civic presence, asserting collective control over public space and property as Robinson, Marquand, and others predicted they would.

Manhattan Bridge Arch and Plaza

Within ten years, the firm of Carrère & Hastings was able to more completely and permanently integrate grandeur with infrastructure in its arch and colonnade framing the Manhattan Bridge Plaza (fig. 6).[18] Reminiscent of the projecting colonnades of Baroque palaces and Bernini's Vatican forecourt, this monumental entry marked the bridge entrance while making physically tangible the 1898 consolidation of Manhattan and Brooklyn into Greater New York. By connecting the new metropolis into a cohesive visual and infrastructural whole, and focusing views down both Chrystie and Canal Streets, Carrère & Hastings realized a City Beautiful monumental node with an arch punctuating visual termini.[19]

The design of the Manhattan Bridge evolved tumultuously over twenty years and four mayoral administra-

Fig. 6. Manhattan Bridge Arch and Plaza by Carrère & Hastings, 1910, as seen today. Modeled on the Porte Saint-Denis in Paris, this monumental infrastructure project evokes the symbolism of historic triumphal arches and marks the interconnection of the boroughs of Manhattan and Brooklyn.

tions,[20] but the conception of a coordinated infrastructure system and City Beautiful monumentality inhered in the project from its beginnings. For example, the *New York Times* reported that the 1899 design would include "a fine opportunity for a grand entrance," perhaps "including a proposed avenue from Union Square directly to the entrance of the new bridge."[21] The *Times* clearly anticipated that the Manhattan Bridge approach would bring to fruition the potential suggested by Dewey Arch and its relationship to the city's spatial form.

The construction of the Manhattan Bridge approach facilitated the City Beautiful by demolishing several blocks of older buildings, clearing the site for the classically inspired arch (fig. 7). By condemning numerous blocks for the bridge entry, anchorage, and extension in 1901, the city ensured enough space for Carrère & Hastings's later neo-Baroque ensemble.[22] Bridge builders' authority ended at the bridge terminus, however, so the city lacked the power to extend the approach into the city as the *Times* had predicted;[23] the City Beautiful ideal of broad avenues radiating out from the arch and plaza ends

abruptly at the corner of the Bowery and Canal Street. The structural arches of the Manhattan Bridge anchorages similarly exert a limited classicizing presence over the neighborhoods razed for bridge construction (fig. 8). Like the Manhattan Bridge Plaza, these massive arches assert municipal presence,[24] but they do not integrate with radial street systems, and so they reflect tension between City Beautiful aspirations and the persistent urban fabric, as did the Dewey Arch before them.

The Manhattan Bridge Arch continued to perpetuate the idea of monumental infrastructural extension, however. In 1912, Manhattan Borough President George McAneny announced a plan for a new boulevard to connect the proposed civic center, north of City Hall Park, with the Manhattan Bridge Plaza (fig. 10).[25] This plan addressed circulation and congestion, combining public grandeur with street systems to create a traffic loop between the Brooklyn and Manhattan Bridges. The boulevard would have been anchored by both the triumphal Manhattan Bridge Arch and the prominent civic arch at McKim, Mead & White's Municipal Building.

PLATE 12

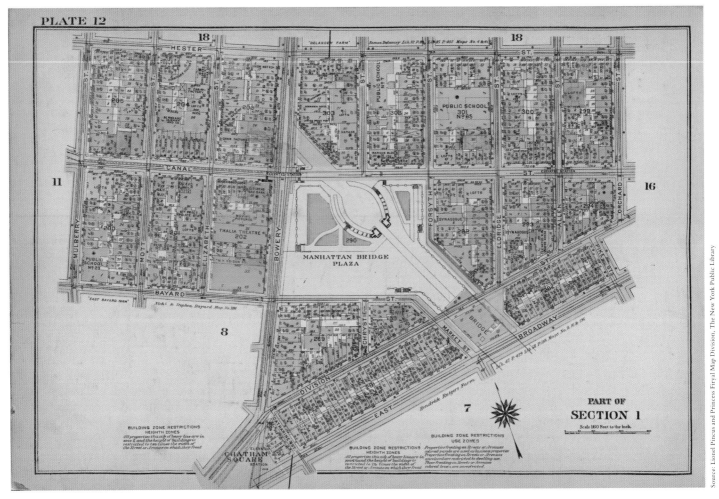

Fig. 7. From *Manhattan Land Book of the City of New York* by G. W. Bromley, 1923. Plate 12, showing Manhattan Bridge Plaza in an area cleared by the city. The site is bounded by the Bowery and Canal, Bayard, and Forsyth Streets.

This proposed boulevard also fulfilled City Beautiful ambitions to renew the city, recalling Marquand's vision for the Washington Arch in Greenwich Village. McAneny predicted that the new street "will wipe up some of the worst buildings in the city and will so raise the value of those adjoining them that the old rookeries will be demolished for modern business structures."[26] McAneny and others supporting the boulevard envisioned more than a monumental infrastructure solution asserting collective identity and raising property values, however. The *Times* anticipated that the boulevard would result in the "wiping out of sordid Chinatown,"[27] suggesting how the City Beautiful functioned as a strategy for social control as well as for technical and aesthetic reform. Indeed, many have interpreted the City Beautiful to be a prescriptive ethical program, evident here in an attempt to replan the city's social topography.[28]

Arches, Axiality, and Identity

Triumph and commemoration returned to Madison Square in 1919 with Thomas Hastings's Victory Arch, another ephemeral manifestation of civic presence at Madison Square (fig. 9).[29] Like the other temporary or unbuilt projects examined here, the Victory Arch suggested an urban focus on points of positional magnificence. As with the world's fairs of the late nineteenth and early twentieth centuries, these projects could not be translated directly into American cities, but they expressed a powerful, recurring ideal that found incremental expression in later planning. The aspirations vested in the arches studied here—to stabilize neighborhood development, to promote collective cooperation, and to physically connect the city—continued to concern planners of the next generation. The City Practical rejected the classical idiom, but it incorporated the aims of

Fig. 8. Looking east on Cherry Street toward the arch in the anchorage of the Manhattan Bridge.

Fig. 9. Victory Arch, Fifth Avenue at Madison Square Park, by Thomas Hastings, 1919. Hastings's design for this temporary arch recalls the triple-arch monuments of ancient Rome.

Fig. 10. *Proposed Boulevard from City Hall to Manhattan Bridge*, drawing by H. M. Pettit, 1914–15. This unbuilt proposal treats the area around the bridge terminus as a formal garden recalling Baroque models, but disconnected from the adjacent urban fabric. Published postcard versions of this drawing suggest City Beautiful ideas had entered the popular imagination.

Source: Lionel Pincus and Princess Firyal Map Division, The New York Public Library

Fig. 11. From *Atlas of the Borough of Manhattan*, Desk Edition, by G. W. Bromley. Plate 31, showing the axial orientation of the arch relative to Fifth Avenue; the picturesque plan of park pathways; and a fountain located at the center of park, off the Fifth Avenue axis.

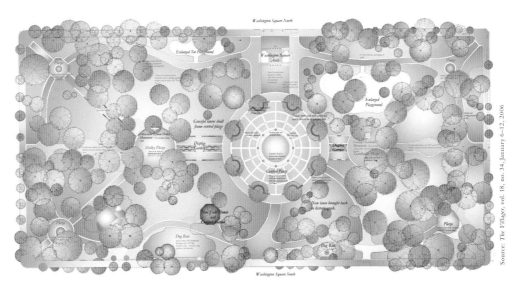

Source: *The Villager*, vol. 18, no. 34, January 6–12, 2006

Fig. 12. Washington Square Park as redesigned by the New York City Parks Department landscape architect George Vellonakis, 2005–08. This plan extends the Fifth Avenue axis into the park, aligning the fountain with the arch and introducing cross-axes defined by statuary aligned with the east and west sides of the fountain.

these arches, realizing their potential through different means. As the aesthetic-infrastructural approaches of the City Beautiful gave way to tools like zoning codes, land use plans, and housing reforms, monumentality became less relevant as a way to assert order and spatial control in American cities.

We might then conclude that New York's arches waned in relevance with the rise of the "disciplinary order of planning."[30] But we can still perceive the power of monumentality to define identity today, in the conflict over redesigning Washington Square Park between 2005 and 2008 (figs. 11, 12).[31] Throughout its history, Washington Square has retained traces of its mid-nineteenth-century picturesque landscape plan, despite the classicizing presence of its arch. The 2005 Parks Department plan to align the fountain with the axis formed by Fifth Avenue and the Washington Arch revived City Beautiful aspirations to formally plan by integrating urban elements into systems of physical and visual order. Many local residents and park users strongly opposed to the plan, however, arguing that the "formal nature of the design … fundamentally altered the park's casual, democratic character."[32] For these critics, the existing, irregular relationship between arch and fountain more faithfully represented the diverse character of Greenwich Village than did the axis proposed by the city. This recurring contest between axial order and eclectic urbanism reminds us that tensions between monumentality and city fabric, or between urban form and process, remain relevant in building twenty-first-century cities.

Jon Ritter is Clinical Associate Professor in the Department of Art History, Urban Design and Architecture Studies at New York University. His research and teaching focus on the origins of urban planning in the United States and Europe, particularly the City Beautiful movement and the early twentieth-century development of American civic centers. Ritter also co-directs New York University's M.A. in Historical and Sustainable Architecture, a London-based program focusing on historic preservation and adaptive reuse.

Notes

1. On the American Renaissance as a collaboration among artists and architects to define American identity through Renaissance-Roman forms, see Richard Guy Wilson and Brooklyn Museum, *The American Renaissance, 1876–1917* (New York: Brooklyn Museum and Pantheon Books, 1979), 11–21. On the American Renaissance and City Beautiful planning, see Robert A. M. Stern, Gregory Gilmartin, and John Massengale, *New York 1900: Metropolitan Architecture and Urbanism 1890–1915* (New York: Rizzoli, 1983), 17–22.

2. Stern, Gilmartin, and Massengale, *New York 1900,* 27–34.

3. Lewis Mumford, *The City in History: Its Origins, Its Transformations, and Its Prospects* (New York: Harcourt, Brace, and World, 1961), 404.

4. Mel Scott, *American City Planning since 1890* (Berkeley and Los Angeles: University of California Press, 1969), 57–60.

5. Elizabeth Macaulay-Lewis, "Triumphal Washington, New York City's First 'Roman Arch,'" in *War as Spectacle: Ancient and Modern Perspectives on the Display of Armed Conflict,* ed. Anastasia Bakogianni and Valerie M. Hope (London: Bloomsbury Academic, 2015), 221.

6. Ibid., 220–23; Stern, Gilmartin, and Massengale, *New York 1900,* 123.

7. Charles Mulford Robinson, *Modern Civic Art, or, the City Made Beautiful* (New York: Putnam, 1918), 226.

8. William R. Stewart, *The History of the Washington Arch in Washington Square, New York, Including the Ceremonies of Laying the Corner-Stone and the Dedication* (New York: Ford and Garnet, Publishers, 1896), 78.

9. Roy Rosenzweig and Elizabeth Blackmar, *The Park and the People: A History of Central Park* (New York: H. Holt and Co., 1994), 131–32.

10. Stern, Gilmartin, and Massengale, *New York 1900,* 132-34.

11. Wilson and Brooklyn Museum, *The American Renaissance,* 87.

12. Robinson, *Modern Civic Art,* 363.

13. On the conflicts between individualism and collectivism in the City Beautiful, see, for example, Thomas S. Hines, "The City Beautiful in American Urban Planning, 1890–1920," *Transactions* 7 (1985): 31; John Brisben Walker, "The City of the Future: A Prophecy, " *The Cosmopolitan,* 31 (1901): 474.

14. Wilson and Brooklyn Museum, *The American Renaissance,* 87–92.

15. See, for example, Henry James, *The American Scene* (London: Chapman and Hall, 1907), 77.

16. Gregory F. Gilmartin, *Shaping the City: New York and the Municipal Art Society* (New York: Clarkson Potter, 1995), 43.

17. Scott, *American City Planning since 1890,* 110–83.

18. Mark Alan Hewitt et al., *Carrère & Hastings Architects,* vol. 1 (New York: Acanthus Press, 2006), 212–20; Gilmartin, *Shaping the City,* 121–27; Stern, Gilmartin, and Massengale, *New York 1900,* 52–54.

19. Note that the Chrystie Street vista was greatly strengthened by the widening of the street in the 1920s and '30s. See Gilmartin, *Shaping the City,* 296.

20. Ibid., 123–28; Hewitt et al., *Carrère & Hastings Architects,* 212–20.

21. The *Times* refers to the design of Bridge Commissioner John L. Shea. See "New York's Proposed Improvements," *New York Times Illustrated Magazine,* September 3, 1899, 7.

22. "Approach for Bridge," *New York Times,* March 16, 1901, 9; "Manhattan Bridge: Clearing Ground for the Approaches Almost Completed," *New-York Tribune,* August 2, 1908, C7.

23. Robert Caro, *The Power Broker: Robert Moses and the Fall of New York* (New York: Alfred A. Knopf, 1974), 392–94.

24. Hewitt et al., *Carrère & Hastings Architects,* 214–15.

25. "To Invite Designs for Court House," *New York Times,* May 28, 1912, 7; "M'aneny Has Bigger Civic Centre Plan," *New York Times,* February 21, 1913, 22.

26. "To Invite Designs for Court House," 7.

27. "Calls Court House Mad Extravagance," *New York Times,* June 14, 1915, 13.

28. See, for example, M. Christine Boyer, *Dreaming the Rational City: The Myth of American City Planning* (Cambridge, MA: MIT Press, 1983), 56.

29. Hewitt et al., *Carrère & Hastings Architects,* 244–46.

30. Boyer, *Dreaming the Rational City,* 57–136.

31. Graham Bowley, "The Battle of Washington Square," *New York Times,* November 21, 2008, CY1.

32. Ibid.

"AN OLD MOTIVE"

NEW YORK'S RESIDENTIAL RENAISSANCE

MARK ALAN HEWITT

Every citizen has two homes: one comes from nature, the other by the state; one from locality and the other, law.
—Marcus Tullius Cicero

Their names are synonymous with the heart and soul of the city: Rockefeller, Morgan, Whitney, Astor, Carnegie. It is easy to forget that, in addition to founding great business and cultural institutions, New York's twentieth-century merchant princes were at the center of a building boom that produced the magnificent palaces on Fifth Avenue (now gone), townhouses on the Upper East Side, nine hundred country houses on Long Island, and many other houses in Westchester County, New Jersey's Somerset Hills, and Connecticut's Long Island Sound "watering holes." In short, they created the largest collection of modern urban and country houses anywhere in the world.[1]

Many were the work of a trusted family architect, who might also be involved in commercial projects. In this they resembled nothing more than the celebrated palazzo-villa commissions given to Andrea Palladio by the Valmarana, Thiene, and Barbaro families in the Veneto.[2] Renaissance partnerships between patron and architect extended to the development of the countryside around the city-state; in New York, plutocrats installed their families in country houses, where sons and daughters socialized and matches were made. From this web of social liaisons, the city grew more prosperous and powerful.

Not all of the architects who worked on these domestic commissions are well known today, but all were highly influential among New York's elite business leaders. Charles Adams Platt, who studied Italian villas assiduously before becoming an architect and

garden designer, embarked on projects in New York with the same ideals as his Renaissance counterparts, often joining his clients in their summer sojourns (fig. 2). Stanford White collaborated with his close friend, Augustus Saint Gaudens, on city and country residences that they and their families enjoyed, often

New York's twentieth-century merchant princes . . . created the largest collection of modern urban and country houses anywhere in the world.

together. Thomas Hastings joined his father-in-law aboard his yacht, the *Oneida*, on trips far and wide. It isn't far-fetched to suggest that these architects were emulating the customs of Cicero, Pliny, and Catullus.

Originally trained as a painter, Platt did his earliest work near Aspet, the Saint Gaudens property in Cornish, New Hampshire, where the New York attorney Charles C. Beaman had purchased land for a summer resort colony in 1881. He worked both as an architect and a garden designer, spending a good deal of each summer at his own country house in the colony. As landscape historians Alma Gilbert and Judith Tankard have observed, the houses and gardens at Cornish were among the most accomplished examples of domestic landscape design in America at the turn of the century, and every member of the colony was dedicated to "garden art." In fact, the founder originally called it "Little New York," envisioning a kind of satellite atelier for the city's cultural leaders, including

Fig. 1. Aerial view of Avalon, Robert Brewster's estate in Mount Kisco, New York, by Delano & Aldrich, 1910, photographed ca. 1932–34.

Fig. 2. Villa Lante, Bagnaia, Lazio, Italy. Casino parterre, photographed 1925.

Fig. 3. Frederick Lee house, 125 East 65th Street, New York, by Charles Adams Platt, 1904.

Fig. 4. Frederick Lee house. Library interior from *Monograph of the Work of Charles Adams Platt* (1913).

Fig. 5 H.A.C. Taylor house, East 71st Street, New York, by McKim, Mead & White, 1894–96.

Fig. 6. H.A.C. Taylor house, Newport, Rhode Island, by McKim, Mead & White, 1882.

painters, writers, architects, and elite business figures.[3] Painters Thomas Dewing and Maxfield Parrish were both central figures in the colony, where theatrical "masques" were often performed outdoors, in classical costumes, to evoke the spirit of Greece, Rome, and the Renaissance. During the summer months, they partook in a *villegiatura*—a country holiday.

Although Platt designed only a few New York townhouses, one of his first was a Colonial Revival residence in 1904 for Frederick Lee at 125 East Sixty-fifth Street (figs. 3–4). Lee, a doctor, subsequently commissioned a country house in Woodstock, Vermont, from his architect, not unlike those at Cornish, where he could retreat during the summer or fall. In the city, Platt found ways to integrate his client's chemistry laboratory and offices with a fully functioning, classically planned terraced house.

Departing from the more typical adjacent brownstones with raised first floors, Lee's house had no stoop, but rather admitted guests directly into a stair hall–vestibule that led up to the formal rooms, accessible by a central, skylit staircase with some features of an Italian palazzo *cortile*. The generous width of the house allowed for a large front drawing room and a dining room facing a backyard garden. The main room, a library, faced the street with three large windows fronting a wrought-iron balcony. It self-consciously resembled the "studiolo" of an Italian nobleman. At just four stories, the house did not adopt the common six-story, attenuated model of its neighbors, and had no bays, turrets, or massive projecting cornices. It was, as architectural historian Keith N. Morgan has suggested, full of surprising innovations.[4]

The Lee house would have pleased Montgomery Schuyler, who decried both the dreary brownstones and the opulent Chateau-style houses springing up on the East Side above Sixtieth Street after 1900.[5] As the "new New York" houses replaced those of the "millionaire district" on Fifth Avenue, architects such as Charles McKim, Thomas Hastings, and William Adams Delano were shaping the streets off Central Park with integrated classical houses, designed not as freestanding symbols of power but as contributors to the fabric of a modern city. In this, they were part of a tradition dating back to

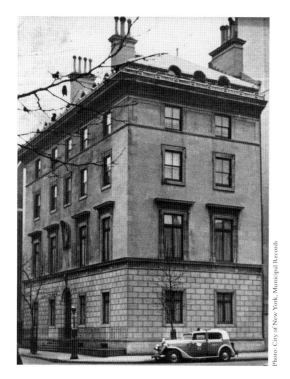

Fig. 7. Robert Brewster house, East 70th Street, New York, by Delano & Aldrich, 1907.

Fig. 8. Avalon, Mount Kisco, New York, by Delano & Aldrich, 1910. Exterior. Designed for Robert Brewster.

Alberti, Raphael, Giulio Romano, and the Renaissance masters who inspired McKim to found the American Academy in Rome in 1895.

McKim's Renaissance-inspired house for H.A.C. Taylor (1894–96), on East Seventy-first Street, followed the architect's groundbreaking Colonial Revival "cottage" in Newport, Rhode Island, constructed in 1882 for Taylor's family (figs. 5, 6). The house for John Innes Kane (1904–06) on Fifth Avenue quoted Florentine and Roman precedents, while Stanford White looked to Baldassare Longhena's Ca' Rezzonico on the Grand Canal in Venice for the basic parti and facade elements of the Joseph Pulitzer house on Seventy-third Street (1901–03). The latter three held tight to the street wall established by earlier houses, while also suggesting a cornice height and rhythm for subsequent neighbors. Their stone and stucco details were restrained compared with many pompous French-inspired houses nearby.[6]

McKim trained Hastings and Hastings trained Delano, although all three spent time at the Ecole des Beaux-Arts in Paris honing their skills. One of the first lessons they learned was that a city should be made with houses that form streets and squares, hiding their private functions behind facades that obey the larger order of the civic realm. It is sometimes hard to see this in the jumbled, seesaw fabric of today's Manhattan, but on many residential streets around Central Park one can sense a connection to Paris, Rome, London, and ultimately, the *palazzo*.[7]

William Adams Delano and his partner, Chester Holmes Aldrich, were often charged with designing multiple houses for their best clients. They even published a small pamphlet on lifestyle preferences that was presented to a house client prior to beginning the project. New clients were asked to answer a set of questions at the end of the booklet. This ensured that each house would be tailored to the individual owner.[8]

Robert S. Brewster commissioned a city house from Delano & Aldrich in 1907, one block south of the Elihu Root house (Carrère & Hastings, 1901) on the corner of East Seventieth Street and Park Avenue (fig. 7). Its facade and general disposition come from a study of Roman *palazzi* of the sixteenth century, although it probably got its parti from Carrère & Hastings's earlier experiments in classical planning.[9] Brewster built a country house with the firm shortly afterward that had a similar classical dignity and discipline.

Fig 9. Avalon, garden "room" with trellis.

Avalon, as the house was called, was nestled in the hills near the town of Mount Kisco, some fifty miles north of the city (fig. 8). Brewster and his family lived simply, without the pretense of a John D. Rockefeller or Otto H. Kahn, two of the firm's most notable country house clients. The house was a "portrait" of its owner, as Delano liked to call many of his domestic works—elegant but not overwhelming. Ellen Shipman designed the large oval garden on axis with the rear ell of the house, no doubt taking some cues from Delano, who dabbled in landscape design. Built in 1910, it was featured in Samuel Howe's *American Country Houses of To-day* (1915) (fig. 10).[10]

Photo: Avery Architectural & Fine Arts Library, Columbia University

Like many other observers, Howe was taken by the seamless integration between the Brewster house and its hilltop surroundings (see fig. 1). None of its three wings were completely visible from one another, and each had a different garden vista. A large loggia faced south, relating to the lower, oval water garden. The formal north front addressed a *pat d'oie* (goosefoot) of allées leading to the Temple of Love in the upper forest. The L-shaped upper terrace faced west and was surrounded by trees to form an outdoor room (fig. 9). Even more sophisticated than a typical Platt house and garden, Avalon used many of the conventions of hilltop villas—multiple levels, water moving from building to garden and back again, wild versus cultured spaces. It also had a tennis court and a pool pavilion to go with its stable and carriage barn.[11]

Following World War I, building slowed a bit on New York's Upper East Side, but its character remained distinctive, cast by the dominant architects of what has been called the American Renaissance.[12] Giants like Charles McKim, Stanford White, John M. Carrère, and Richard Morris Hunt were gone, but they left a legacy of students and apprentices. None in this younger generation created a larger group of city and country houses than Mott B. Schmidt.

Schmidt was an apprentice with Carrère & Hastings before starting a practice in Manhattan after the war. Like Delano, he favored the crisp, understated qualities of brick Georgian architecture when designing a townhouse for a client like Clarence Dillon on East Eightieth Street. Built in 1929 for Dillon-Bigelow Realty, this house was wider than typical, and had an

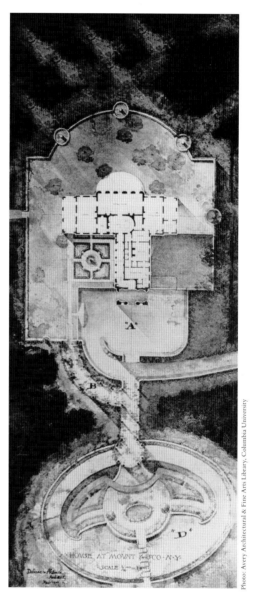

Fig. 10. Avalon. Site plan. Published in *Samuel Howe, American Country Houses of To-Day* (1915).

Photo: Avery Architectural & Fine Arts Library, Columbia University

extra story for servants' accommodations behind its unusual pediment (fig. 12).[13] The beautiful, English-inspired doorway is the focus of the facade, as was often the case in Schmidt's townhouses. During the 1920s, Dillon, Read & Company was a leader in the nascent field of investment banking. Founder Clarence Dillon came to New York from Texas, choosing Schmidt for a group of projects that ranged from New Jersey to Maine.

Dillon purchased a large parcel of prime farmland in the Somerset Hills of central New Jersey just south of James Cox Brady's Hamilton Farm, intending to develop his own horse farm there. The Essex Hounds had just moved west to establish fox hunting in the area, and equestrian trails had been well developed by neighbors such as Ledyard Blair and Percy Rivington Pyne. What became known as the Mountain Colony came to rival Long Island and Westchester County as a watering hole for New Yorkers.[14]

Dillon's first and largest house, Dunwalke Farm, was a Georgian manor designed by Cross & Cross. Like Brady, Dillon seemed initially more concerned with size than with quality in his domicile, as his architects produced a somewhat clumsy amalgam of classical details on a boxy mass of brick. By 1936, however, he went to Schmidt for a second house, probably intended for himself but soon passed on to his son, C. Douglas Dillon. In this Palladian, five-part country house, Schmidt achieved the kind of tasteful balance of proportion, detail, and massing that would have impressed a Renaissance architect (fig. 11).

Dunwalke East, as the house was called, is a fitting bookend to McKim's H.A.C. Taylor house of 1882 in

Fig. 11. Dunwalke East, Far Hills, New Jersey, by Mott B. Schmidt, 1936. Designed for Clarence Dillon. Facade and entry court.

Newport. Whereas McKim studied American colonial precedents on an 1877 sketching trip with his partners before embarking on the first classically inspired house of its time, Schmidt had decades of examples to draw from prior to designing for Dillon in Far Hills. He could even quote from himself, fashioning the doorway for this house after the earlier one in Manhattan. Like his idol, Palladio, Schmidt linked an urban facade to a rustic, country facade in this pairing of a palazzo and villa for modern New Yorkers.

The plan of the house combined the proportional rigor of a Palladian villa with the functional intricacies of a twentieth-century residence. The ballroom was generously sized for entertaining, but also had a hidden room for services such as radios and, eventually, television equipment. Each bedroom had its own suite with a bath, closet, and often a separate vestibule (fig. 16). The semicircular staircase included notable innovations; it was constructed without intermediate support, using steel as a stiffener for the wooden stringers, and placed outside the main block or entry hall in one of the hyphens connecting the side wings (fig. 17).

The modernity of the house is apparent in the spare use of ornament and uniformity of the brick

Fig. 12. Clarence Dillon house, East 80th Street, New York, by Mott B. Schmidt, 1929.

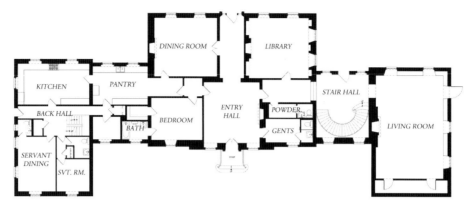

Fig. 15. Dunwalke East. First-floor plan.

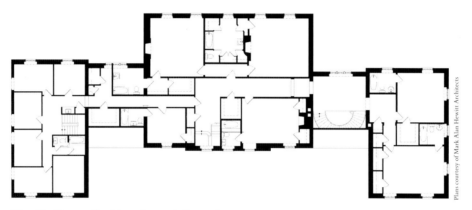

Fig. 16. Dunwalke East. Second-floor plan.

Plans courtesy of Mark Alan Hewitt Architects

walls, which define the three main masses precisely, as if chiseled from a block of marble. The only flourishes occur in the main cornice and the two main doorways, one with a segmental pediment, the other triangular (fig. 18). The latter features a Palladian Ionic entablature over Scamozzi-style capitals in carved wood. The interior of the entry hall continues this theme, much as in a typical villa in the Veneto by Palladio or Scamozzi. By the time Schmidt closed his New York office in the 1950s, there were no more commissions for East Side townhouses, which had given way to the elegant apartment blocks that define the neighborhoods around Central Park today. Schmidt did, however, design a number of large country houses throughout the United States for families like the Fords and Bronfmans. In this way, he brought the tradition of villa and palazzo architecture full circle.

New York's master builders of the early twentieth century were aware of not only their role in the city's financial expansion but also their part in shaping the moral and political life of the *polis*—as the Greeks or Romans would have seen their society and its citizens. Full members of a just society were compelled to make their homes in the city, and outside it, in order to perform their civic roles. They understood that living well was not merely a social necessity, but also an art. When we assess the finest examples of domestic architecture—in both city and country—New York's master architects should take their place among the leading artists of the "American century," no less than their colleagues in music, literature, painting, sculpture, and drama. Without them, New York would not be the cultural capital that it is today.

Mark Alan Hewitt, FAIA, is an architect, preservationist, and historian practicing in Bernardsville, New Jersey. His books include *The Architect and the American Country House, Gustav Stickley's Craftsman Farms*, and the two-volume monograph *Carrère & Hastings Architects* (with Charles Warren, Kate Lemos, and William Morrison). He currently teaches in the Department of Art History, Rutgers University, New Brunswick. Hewitt received the Arthur Ross Award for writing and criticism from the ICAA in 2008.

Fig. 17. Dunwalke East stair hall.

Fig. 18. Dunwalke East doorway.

Notes

"A very old motive" comes from Henry James's preface (1902) to *The Wings of the Dove* (London: Folio Society, 2005), xiii. James refers to archetypal stories in fiction, though he might well be referring to the desire of Americans to emulate their European counterparts in manners, dress, and culture.

1. Mark Alan Hewitt, *The Architect and the American Country House: 1890–1940* (New Haven: Yale University Press, 1990) has a comprehensive history of this era's country houses.

2. Andrea Palladio (1508–80) was among the most successful Renaissance architects. Many of his patrons commissioned more than one house from the architect. One of the best biographies is James S. Ackerman's *Palladio* (Harmondsworth, UK: Penguin, 1966).

3. See Alma M. Gilbert and Judith B. Tankard, *A Place of Beauty: The Artists and Gardens of the Cornish Colony* (Berkeley, CA: Ten Speed Press, 2000), 41–55.

4. Keith N. Morgan, *Charles A. Platt: The Artist as Architect* (Cambridge, MA: MIT Press; and New York: Architectural History Foundation, 1985): 131–34.

5. Montgomery Schuyler, "The New New York House," *Architectural Record 19* (February 1906): 83–103. See also Herbert Croly, "The Contemporary New York Residence," *Architectural Record* 12 (December 1902): 705–22.

6. Leland M. Roth, *McKim, Mead & White Architects* (New York: Harper & Row, 1983); *Samuel G. White, McKim, Mead & White, The Masterworks* (New York: Rizzoli, 2003).

7. Charles Lockwood, *Bricks and Brownstone: The New York Rowhouse, 1783–1929,* 2nd ed. (New York: Rizzoli, 2003).

8. See, for example, Chester B. Price, *Portraits of Ten Country Houses Designed by Delano & Aldrich* (Garden City, NY: Doubleday Page: 1924), and Mark Alan Hewitt, "Domestic Portraits: The Early Long Island Country Houses of Delano & Aldrich," in Joanna Krieg, ed., *Long Island Architecture* (Hempstead, NY: Long Island Studies Institute, 1991), 98–115.

9. Robert A. M. Stern, Gregory Gilmartin, and John Massengale, *New York 1900* (New York: Rizzoli, 1983), 324. See also William Adams Delano, "No. 100 East 70th Street," *New York Architect* 2 (January 1908).

10. Peter Pennoyer and Anne Walker, *The Architecture of Delano and Aldrich* (New York: Norton, 2003), and *Samuel Howe, American Country Houses of To-Day* (New York: Architectural Book Publishing Co., 1915): 118–23.

11. Judith B. Tankard, *The Gardens of Ellen Biddle Shipman* (New York: Sagapress and Harry N. Abrams, 1996), 91–93. The author acknowledges that the basic layout was by Delano.

12. See Richard Guy Wilson and Diane Pilgrim, eds., *The American Renaissance 1876–1917* (New York: Pantheon, 1979).

13. See Mark Alan Hewitt, *The Architecture of Mott B. Schmidt* (New York: Rizzoli, 1991).

14. See John K. Turpin and W. Barry Thomson, *New Jersey Country Houses: The Somerset Hills,* 2 vols. (Far Hills, NJ: Mountain Colony Press, 2004 and 2006).

CHORAGIC MONUMENT OF LYSICRATES
ATHENS AUG.17.1879

F.H.B

EDUCATION AND PRACTICE
ARCHITECTURAL DRAWINGS AT THE AVERY LIBRARY

JANET PARKS

Architecture as a creative profession attracts those who are dedicated to the education and the continuing sharpening of the mind. In the late nineteenth century, there were few academic architecture schools in the United States, but there were ample opportunities for architectural education itself, through lectures, ateliers, and professional societies. When the young architect Henry Ogden Avery, the second son of the well-respected and prosperous New York art dealer Samuel Putnam Avery, died on April 30, 1890, his family memorialized him by donating his library of two thousand books and his architectural drawings to Columbia College. They continued to support the Avery Memorial Library, as it was then known, with funds for books and a new McKim, Mead & White-designed building in 1912.

Opposite page: Fig. 1. Francis Henry Bacon, Choragic Monument of Lysicrates (Athens, Greece), August 17, 1879. Graphite and wash on paper, 14 3/4 x 9 in.

Fig. 2. Ogden Codman, Edgemere (Newport, Rhode Island), alterations and additions: [interior elevation of passage to new dining hall], [1895 to 1896]. Watercolor and graphite on paper, 18 5/8 x 26 5/8 in.

GREEK IONIC ORDER.

Fig. 3. Katherine Lines, Greek Ionic order, [18]96. Graphite, ink, and wash on paper, 33 ½ x 23 in.

Fig. 4. Harold Van Buren Magonigle, night view (Paestum, Italy), from Rotch Traveling Fellowship, [1894 to 1896]. Watercolor on board, 11 ½ x 14 ½ in.

The images reproduced here demonstrate the range of drawings at Avery, collected in the 127 years since the library was founded. Two drawings—those of Katherine Lines (fig. 3) and Paul Cret (fig. 10)—are academic work, done at the New England School of Applied Design for Women and the Ecole des Beaux-Arts, respectively, evidence of a shared educational philosophy. Those by Francis Bacon (fig. 1) and Harold Van Buren Magonigle (fig. 4) are a reminder of the value of travel for the continuing refreshment of the mind, both architecturally and creatively. The drawing of the house for William Fahnestock in Katonah by Charles Platt (fig. 6) is a plate from the architect's 1913 monograph—a unified format he used to organize the presentation of his domestic work. The remaining drawings range in date from an 1830s townhouse by Alexander Jackson Davis (fig. 7) to a 1990 antefix designed by Kent Bloomer (fig. 9) for the Harold Washington Library Center in Chicago. Interiors and urban projects fill in the chronology, with drawings by architects as diverse as Stanford White, Benjamin Wistar Morris, and Ogden Codman (fig. 2) exploring classical vocabulary.

Architectural imagery is as powerful today as it was for each of these architects, who expressed their ideas through a combination of their hand, study, and imagination. Stanford White (fig. 5) used his own residences in the city and on Long Island as a laboratory for his imagination. Morris's design (fig. 8) for a new Metropolitan Opera

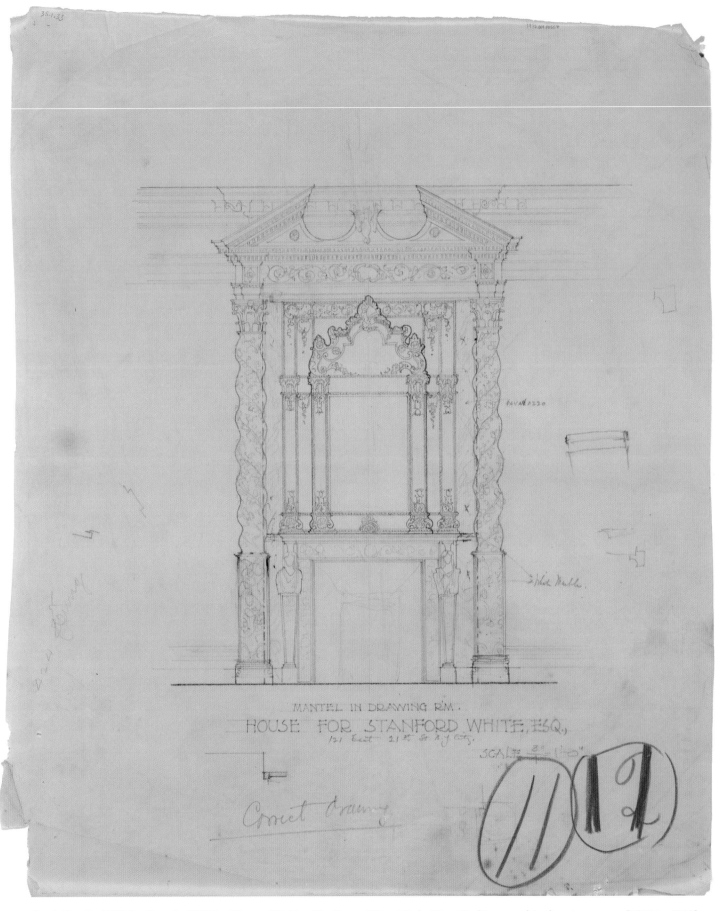

Fig. 5. Stanford White, Stanford White House, 121 East 21st Street (New York, New York): mantel in drawing room, [1894 to 1901]. Graphite on tracing paper, 18 x 15 in.

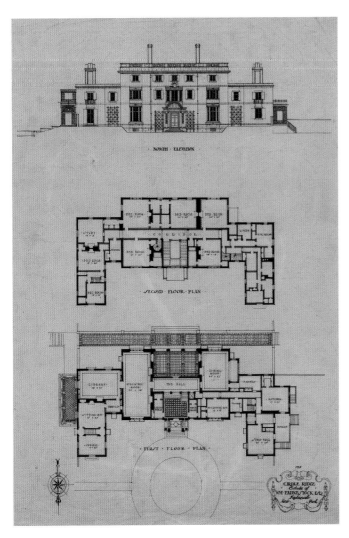

Fig. 6. Charles Platt, William F. Fahnestock and Julia Goetchius residence, Girdle Ridge (Katonah, New York): plans and elevation, 1911. Ink on paper, 22 x 16 in.

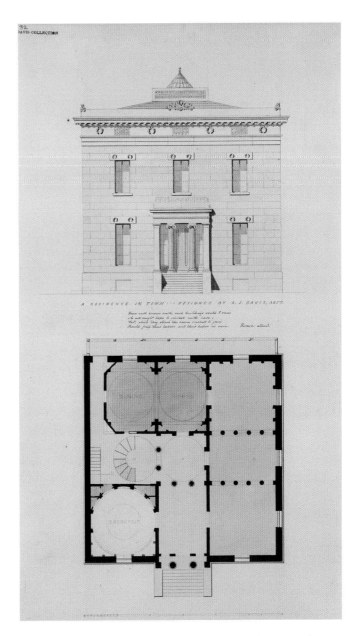

Fig. 7. Alexander Jackson Davis, unidentified townhouse, (New York, New York), [ca. 1835?]. Graphite and wash on paper, 14 x 8 ½ in.

House was not built, but his urban vision influenced the scale and plan of Rockefeller Center. Finally, Bloomer's antefix pays homage to two great Chicago architects: a seedpod to honor Louis Sullivan's organic ornament, and spears and shields in the curtain wall to reference Karl Friedrich Schinkel, who influenced Mies van der Rohe.

The Avery family could not have imagined the growth in collections that its bequest of 1890 has fostered. The book collections of the library number more than 600,000 volumes, including 40,000 rare books. The Drawings & Archives department, boosted by the 2012 acquisition of the Frank Lloyd Wright Foundation Archives (co-owned with the Museum of Modern Art), has holdings of more than two million items, including drawings, photographs, and archival materials. A primary resource for scholar, student, and practitioner alike, today's Avery Architectural & Fine Arts Library strives to fulfill Henry Ogden Avery's ideal for architectural study and inquiry, both in traditional materials and the born-digital collections of the future.

Fig. 8. Benjamin Wistar Morris, (Chester B. Price, delineator), Metropolitan Opera House at Rockefeller Center (New York, New York): aerial view, May 11, 1929. Graphite and charcoal on paper, 24 ¼ x 28 in.

Fig. 9. Kent Bloomer, Chicago Public Library (Chicago, Illinois): antefix on cornice, July 1990. Graphite on paper, 11 x 23 ½ in.

Fig. 10. Paul Cret, meeting room for the Institute of France, Ecole des Beaux-Arts (Paris, France): competition drawing, 1901. Graphite, ink, and wash on paper, 19 x 21 in.

Janet Parks was curator of Drawings and Archives at the Avery Library from 1978 until her retirement in June 2017. During this time, the department made more than 650 acquisitions, including the Frank Lloyd Wright Foundation Archive (co-owned with the Museum of Modern Art), bringing the collection to more than two million items. Parks has curated exhibitions on Max Abramovitz, Ely Jacques Kahn, the Woodlawn Cemetery (with Charles Warren), and the Guastavino Fireproof Construction Company. She has lectured and published on architectural drawings in the Avery collections; her most recent publication is an essay on Frank Lloyd Wright drawings for the catalogue of the 2017 exhibition *Frank Lloyd Wright at 150: Unpacking the Archive*, at the Museum of Modern Art in New York.

STEEL BONES
OF THE NEW YORK PUBLIC LIBRARY

CHARLES D. WARREN

On my first day teaching at the Institute of Classical Architecture & Art in the 1990s, I conducted a tour of Carrère & Hastings's New York Public Library. As I pointed to the abbreviated Doric entablature in the entrance hall, Henry Hope Reed appeared on the mezzanine, as if on cue. Henry had written a book on the building and he reveled in the complex embellishment of its magnificent architecture. When the tour resumed, much to our delight, he took the lead. But the marble and oak surfaces Henry so eloquently described are not the whole story. They envelop a seven-story steel cage, which he barely mentioned. And this ingenious construction, known as "the stacks," not only supports the weight of shelves and floors with capacity for three million books but it also supports the floor of what is today called the Rose Reading Room above them. This vast structure is central to the building's architecture and purpose (fig. 1).[1]

The 1,300 thin steel columns in the stacks are arranged in 4-foot-9-inch by 3-foot rectangular bays riveted to equally thin steel horizontals that support seven floors—1 ½-inch-thick marble slabs—each 7 feet 6 inches apart. It is an intricate three-dimensional grid. The system is the culmination of fifty years of experimentation that can be traced from the first self-supporting iron stacks built in Europe in the middle of the nineteenth century through innovations constructed in America as the twentieth century approached. These ferrous metal (iron and steel) structures were attached to, and sometimes supported, parts of the masonry buildings that enclosed them. They are hybrid constructions related by time, technique, and materials to innovations that gave rise to the skyscraper. But the lavish embellishment of the New York Public Library's marble

walls and its role as the centerpiece of City Beautiful–era New York have led some to overlook the functional and expressive use of these combined materials. The steel bones within the stone walls of the New York Public Library are the genesis of the building's form and purpose; their significance should not be overlooked.

The first iron book stacks were constructed in the central court of the British Museum in 1854–57. Although Sidney Smirke was the architect, Anthony Panizzi, the librarian, was a full partner in their conception.[2] These

The beauty of the reading room and the functional elegance of the stacks are as much felt as seen . . .

stacks were divided into three-story, skylit quadrants with the library's celebrated iron-domed reading room at their center (fig. 2). Iron was considered ideal for the construction of libraries. Its strength allowed for thin columns that left more room for books and thin mullions that made large skylights possible. Iron was also used to cast perforated floor grates, which allowed light to penetrate through them to floors below. All this eliminated the need for illumination with gas, or other flame—it was considered proof against the dangers of fire.

Rapid growth in library collections during the nineteenth century was driven by innovations in printing and binding. This created a need for greatly enlarged shelf capacity, not only in London but also throughout the Atlantic world. In Paris, the long-contemplated expansion of the Bibliothèque Impériale (later Nationale) de France (BnF) was realized in 1868 with a new building designed by Henri Labrouste. It followed his earlier work in iron and stone at the Bibliothèque Sainte-Geneviève of 1851. At BnF, Labrouste gave dramatic expression to the strength of

Fig. 1. Cutaway view of the New York Public Library stacks from *Scientific American*, May 27, 1911.

Fig. 2. One quadrant of Sidney Smirke's British Museum Library stacks (1854–57), showing the curve of the central reading room on the left and daylight from above coming through the iron floor grates.

Fig. 3. Iron stacks of Henri Labrouste's central storeroom at the Bibliothèque Nationale de France (1868), photographed by L.-E. Durandelle in 1888.

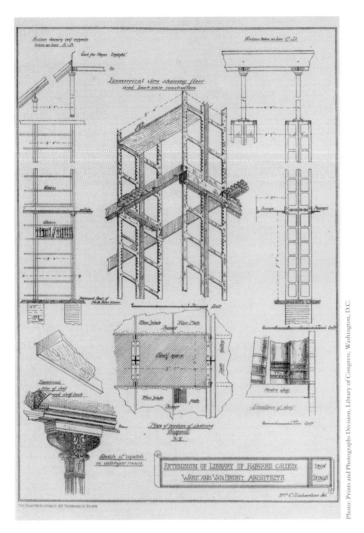

Fig. 4. Details of Ware & Van Brunt's design for the iron stacks in the firm's 1877 addition to Gore Hall Library at Harvard University.

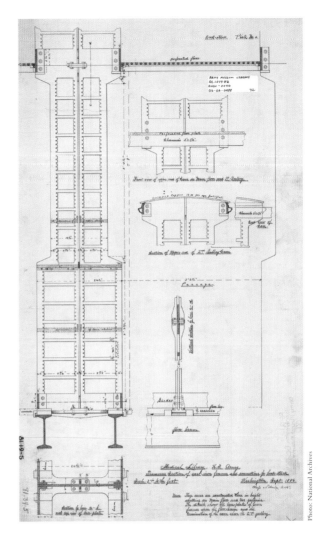

Fig. 5. Detail of the 1886 library stacks design for the Army Medical Museum and Library by Cluss & Schulze Architects.

iron with thin, classically styled columns supporting seemingly weightless, oculus-centered domes.[3] This marvelous room is adjacent to the central storeroom where books were kept in four-story, skylit, iron stacks similar to their British counterparts (fig. 3). Significantly, both French and British national libraries separated books from readers, departing from the traditional arrangement where book-lined walls surrounded the scholars who used them.

Henry Van Brunt was the first American architect to grasp the possibilities of the new iron stacks. In 1879 he wrote, ". . . the provisions made in the British Museum, and by the accomplished M. Labrouste in his late addition to the National Library at Paris are necessarily adapted to the accommodation of certain existing conditions of service, or traditions of practice in those monumental collections. For our own use these precedents can

afford useful hints indeed."[4] Van Brunt, and his partner, William R. Ware, had trained in Richard Morris Hunt's architectural atelier and he also claimed to have worked with Detlef Lienau, a former student of Labrouste who practiced in New York. Either of these men might have inspired Van Brunt's interest in Labrouste's Paris libraries.[5] By 1877, when the firm of Ware & Van Brunt was hired to design a new wing for Harvard's Gore Hall Library, Ware had turned his attention to establishing an architecture program at the Massachusetts Institute of Technology (MIT), so Van Brunt was running the practice.[6] His design for six stories of book stacks (three stories taller than those in Europe) employed "iron skeleton uprights" supporting not only the floors and books but also the concrete roof and its patented skylights (fig. 4). Windows in the side walls of the Gore Hall stacks provided additional illumi-

Fig. 6. Library Hall, Army Medical Museum and Library (1886), with its three-story system of iron stacks and clerestory windows. Photograph taken after removal of the mechanized book lift.

nation, making possible a dense block of shelves separated only by narrow aisles—a far more efficient arrangement than the wide bays used in Europe. When Van Brunt wrote gratefully of the "constant cooperation and advice from the authorities of the University," who enabled him to work "directly toward a practical end," he was referring to Justin Winsor, the first president of the American Library Association, who, like Panizzi in London, exerted a profound influence on the Gore stacks and later American library development.

Librarians such as Panizzi and Winsor played leading roles in devising new methods to store and catalogue growing library collections. Their collaborations with architects were often contentious but resulted in important nineteenth-century library design innovations.[7] John Shaw Billings, the first director of the New York Public Library, was also at the forefront of library innovation. He began his career as a surgeon during the Civil War, and his interest in buildings developed from an effort to improve hospital design (he later produced diagrams for Johns Hopkins Hospital and consulted on its design). After the war, Billings took charge of the Army Medical Library,

where he expanded the collection and devised new methods of indexing and cataloguing it. Eventually, in 1886, when the collection outgrew Ford's theater where it was housed, Billings consulted with architect Adolph Cluss on the construction of a new building for the Army Medical Museum and Library on the Washington Mall.

Billings used the new building to experiment with library organization. As the project progressed, he substituted three-level, self-supporting, iron book stacks with an exposed dumbwaiter in place of the traditional library of galleried, book-lined alcoves proposed by Cluss. Light from clerestory windows penetrated through cast-iron grate floors to supplement illumination from windows on both sides. It was an ungainly piece of mechanized furniture occupying half of the tall, bare reading room two stories above street level (figs. 5, 6). But the elevated location and iron stacks provided the kernel of the idea Billings later cultivated at the New York Public Library.[8]

Construction of the Washington building was supervised by the Army's chief engineer, Thomas L. Casey, assisted by his staff and Bernard R. Green, a civilian engineer. Surely its design influenced these men in the 1890s,

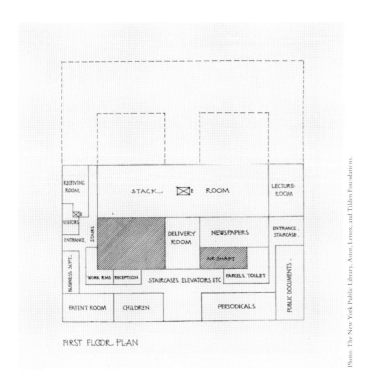

Fig. 7. Plan diagram for the New York Public Library first-stage competition program (1897). William R. Ware refined sketches by John Shaw Billings to produce plan diagrams such as this one for each floor. Dashed lines indicate possible future expansion.

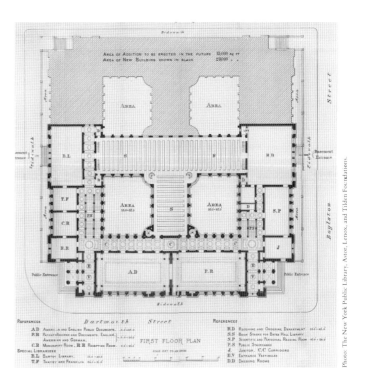

Fig. 8. First-floor plan based on Henry Van Brunt's preliminary study for the Boston Public Library site on Copley Square from *Report on the Fitness of the English High and Latin School Building for the Uses of the Public Library*, 1882. Note the similarities to the plan diagram for the New York Public Library in fig. 7.

when they worked together on the Library of Congress. It was Green who designed and patented the steel stacks there, an ingenious system he modified later for use at the New York Public Library.[9]

Billings's participation in architectural projects often took the form of organizational diagrams; he was concerned with function, not aesthetics. His interest in the mechanics of building systems was pragmatic and scientific and can be seen in his writings on heating and ventilation. In the 1880s, he taught a civil engineering course at Columbia University where William Ware had moved from MIT to found another architecture school.[10] This connection with Van Brunt's former partner and the one he had with Bernard Green would have a significant impact on the design of New York's new library.

After Billings was hired as the first director of the New York Public Library and the site of the obsolete Croton distributing reservoir at Fifth Avenue and Forty-second Street had been secured for the new library, he engaged Ware and Green to join him on a committee to organize a design competition for the library.

The key to Billings's innovation at the New York

Public Library was in the plan diagrams he sketched. The reading room was located on top of a system of seven-story book stacks, which placed it on the building's third floor. This arrangement was made possible by the introduction of electric lights, which eliminated the need for skylights. It had several advantages, but the most notable was the efficiency that resulted from the very short vertical distance between readers and books. Centrally located dumbwaiters exploited this proximity, making book delivery quick and efficient. But it was Ware who interpreted and refined Billings's crude sketches to produce the clear plan diagrams that accompanied the sixteen-page program detailing the competition requirements (fig. 7). Ware had run numerous design competitions and had written about the ethics of their organization; his participation signaled that the competition would be fair and professional.[11] Green's participation sent a signal, too, since locating the reading room over the stacks required the use of his patented steel stacks. This let everyone know that Billings was determined to use this novel and efficient system.

Because locating the reading room so far from the building entrance was controversial, the competition was

Fig. 9. West facade of the New York Public Library seen from West 40th Street.

Fig. 10. South facade of Henri Labrouste's Bibliothèque Sainte-Geneviéve (1838–50).

organized in two stages to test the idea. The first stage was open to all New York architects, and though it required designs that located the reading room over the stacks, competitors were invited to propose alternatives. The results of the first stage satisfied Billings (and the trustees) that the upper-floor location was feasible, so he and Ware made minor adjustments to the program and diagrams for the final competition stage. This was open to six architects selected from the twelve winners of the first stage and six prominent architects who were invited to compete.

Charles F. McKim, of McKim, Mead & White, saw the plan diagrams as a usurpation of the architect's prerogatives, and he resisted accepting the invitation to compete for the commission. His recent experience as architect of the Boston Public Library is likely to have contributed to his wariness. That project, like the New York Public Library, had started as a competition with a detailed program; Boston's was based on schematic plan studies by Henry Van Brunt and years of internal discussion. It called for a pair of light courts and iron book stacks seven stories high (similar to the New York Public Library's requirements) (fig. 8). The winning entry, a design by Charles Atwood, who had begun his career at Ware & Van Brunt, followed the program closely. But after more than a year of political maneuvering, unpaid competition prizes, and indecision, the result was abandoned as

unworkable. McKim was hired in the wake of this failure, and his design, widely acclaimed for its beauty, did not follow the earlier competition program. Librarians, frustrated at having their preferences ignored, complained bitterly about the inefficient storage and delivery of books. This episode was known to all (Billings's papers include a draft of the Boston competition brief), and it served each differently as a cautionary tale.[12] It explains Billings's effort to run an ethical, professional competition and the care he took to enforce his plan. It also explains McKim's reluctance to compete. But McKim's stature caused the trustees to view his participation as critical, so adherence to the plan diagrams was made optional.[13]

John M. Carrère and Thomas Hastings were also invited to compete, and Carrère did not share McKim's misgivings about a detailed program. In 1893, he had written, "… it is necessary, in the first place, that the program be as complete as possible, giving the architect all the information obtainable concerning the requirements of the building, the different spaces, their sizes, how occupied, in what relation to each other they are to be used, … as much, in fact, as will enable the architect to fully understand the purpose of his building and the spirit in which it should be designed."[14]

In the event, Carrère & Hastings won the competition and McKim, Mead & White placed third. Perhaps the younger architects were selected as Carrère had advocated elsewhere, "not for [their] scheme, which should be the program, and which should be furnished for [them] to develop, but for the ability with which [they have] accomplished this development."[15]

The winning design transformed Billings's diagrams. It reflected the Ecole des Beaux-Arts training of the architects and showed, too, that they were current with recent architectural developments in the French capital. But it also demonstrated the architects' interest in new building technique as a component of artistic design. This is especially true where the stacks are given exterior expression on the library's west facade (fig. 9). Carrère & Hastings set aside the all-iron example of Sidney Smirke's London library and looked instead to the libraries of Labrouste. His integration of iron into the masonry-based tradition of classical composition directly influenced the design of the New York Public Library. The new library's west facade, with its repetitive arches, extreme scale shifts, and garland frieze, is the most unconventional part of the building's exterior; it represents the stacks behind it and makes clear reference to Labrouste's facade for the iron and stone Bibliothèque Sainte-Geneviève (fig. 10).

Tall, extraordinarily narrow openings divide the New York Public Library's west facade into twenty-seven pilasters. Their crowded intercolumniation is governed by the proportions of the rolled steel shelves behind them, not the classical orders. This tight spacing makes their identification as pilasters ambiguous; from some vantage points, they appear to be a single wall with windows cut into it. In either case, the thin, flat planes of this part of the facade differentiate the stacks from the more robustly sculptural walls everywhere else. It is as if the organizational idea of

Fig. 11. Steel and cast-iron book stacks at the New York Public Library. This photograph was taken before the marble slab floors were laid into the steel frames that support them, so it is possible to see the three-dimensional grid structure.

the French library—a reading room above a stored collection—has been extruded upward to accommodate the seven-story steel cage and then nestled within the New York Public Library's more complex program. Carrère & Hastings emphasized this greater size and complexity again with the design of small door balconies analogous to Labrouste's small rectangular windows. These openings infuse both facades with a lively play of scale, but the doors at the New York Public Library provide ventilation for the reading room and resolve the syncopation of the odd-numbered arched window bays above with the even-numbered slot window bays below.

Hastings believed contemporary architecture should be a continuation of the then four-hundred-year-old traditions of the Renaissance and he found the stylistic eclecticism of his era absurd, especially when it strayed into the Gothic. But he acknowledged the need for new materials and building techniques—he thought the tradition should evolve.[16] On the subject of tall buildings he wrote, "It would seem as if nature had come forward to provide us with comparatively new materials, in iron and steel, to assist us in this new kind of work. That these materials should play a most important part in our designing, it seems to me must be accepted . . ."[17] Carrère, too, and probably to a greater degree, embraced this new material. He had begun his career mixing iron-trussed roofs with complex skylights and masonry walls to build the first modern panorama buildings in America. Together, these men pioneered other innovations such as exposed concrete and electric lighting. They accepted novelty and gave it expression within the continuous development of architectural tradition.

Carrère & Hastings's design synthesizes a half-century of experiment and experience by integrating systems of shelving, lighting, ventilation, and communication into a complex spatial and structural matrix. It was a collaboration of architects and librarians aware of their place in a continuum. Around the library's utilitarian program, the architects shaped spaces of marble and oak, employing artistic embellishments to dramatize an operatic sequence leading visitors from the street to the magnificent reading room. This spatial construct enveloped, and depended upon, the steel skeleton of the book stacks. In that space, a sublime labyrinth of knowledge, visitors wander within an exposed structural skeleton holding millions of books (fig. 11). It provides a rare chance to experience the kind of steel frame that has come to define New York's architecture. Its mechanized world of steel stands ready to deliver up its treasures to the center of the humanistic world of stone above it. Together, they form a complex choreography—a dance where the reader is a partner to the book.

Fig. 12. Steel and cast-iron circulating library within the New York Public Library now known as the Celeste Bartos Forum.

Photo: Wurts Bros. (New York, NY.)/Museum of the City of New York. X2010.7I.2004

The beauty of the reading room and the functional elegance of the stacks are as much felt as seen, but once lodged in the mind, their ingenious design is not easily forgotten. Ferrous metal is again prominent and visible in another part of the library where its combination with stone serves as a poetic analogue to the pragmatic prose of the stacks. This room, now called the Celeste Bartos Forum, exemplifies the integration of steel and stone that had been on Hastings's mind at least since 1894 when he wrote, "Some practical system should be devised, which would permit the use of apparent iron construction, within the spirit of our laws. We might use exposed iron in a partly decorative way to indicate the constructive members

which are concealed of necessity..."[18] Here, ferrous metal is arched, embellished, and fused with a cast, fragmented, classical order, and the stone is hung in panels that emphatically bear no weight (figs. 12, 13). In the flood of light that pours in through the dramatic domed skylight, the reference to the Grand Palais in Paris is plain and the reversal between steel frame and stone wall is explicit. Like the stacks, the room's light steel frame is distinct from the thick stone walls that surround it. And like the stacks, too, it terminates an axis aligned with a principal entrance to the building.

Carrère & Hastings searched for a modern style of architecture and Hastings wrote of this repeatedly: "Only when we come to realize our true historic position and the principles of continuity in history, when we allow the spirit of our life to be the spirit of our style, recognizing, first of all, that form and all design are the natural outcome of the nature or purpose of the object to be made—only then can we hope to find real style everywhere asserting itself."[19] Yet as these architects searched and experimented, they were, perhaps inadvertently, producing the modern style they saw as elusive. The colossal steel grid at the center of their New York library was a version of the skeletal steel frames that were transforming the city's skyline, and although the library's frame did not support its marble walls, as it frequently did in tall buildings, the interdependence of steel and stone was embedded in the nature and purpose of the library. Moreover, the building's west facade used stone to express the new proportions that steel enforced. Surely these are elements of the "real style" these architects sought.

Henry Hope Reed's book about the New York Public Library and the tours he frequently gave there helped revive interest in the building's grand public rooms and now volunteers lead tours of it several times a day; but they do not include the stacks, where six levels sit idle and empty. Many books, once held there for delivery within minutes, now take days to arrive from their exile in New Jersey. As tourists shuffle through the magnificent rooms, readers must wait patiently for the books to return. Until the empty stacks are once again filled with books, the architectural promise embodied in the tight connection between beauty and structure and purpose remains hollow.

Charles D. Warren is an architect whose New York–based firm has completed projects across the United States. In addition to his practice, he writes about architecture and its history. Warren is co-author of *The Architecture of Carrère & Hastings* and *Sylvan Cemetery*, which he also co-edited. His essays introduce new editions of *The Architecture of Charles A. Platt* and *New Towns for Old*. He is a graduate of Skidmore College (B.S. in fine art) and Columbia University (M.Arch). Warren was the Muschenheim Fellow at the University of Michigan and served as Town Architect in Seaside, Florida.

Photo: © Peter Aaron/OTTO

Fig. 13. Steel and cast-iron detail of the Celeste Bartos Forum at the New York Public Library.

Notes

1. Henry H. Reed, *The New York Public Library* (New York: Norton, 1986).

2. Esdaile Arundel, *The British Museum Library* (London: Allen & Unwin, 1946).

3. Corinne Belier, Barry Bergdoll, and Marc Le Coeur, eds., *Henri Labrouste: Structure Brought to Light* (New York: The Museum of Modern Art, 2013). An excellent series of essays on Labrouste and his libraries.

4. Henry Van Brunt, "Library Buildings," untitled written remarks in *The Library Journal* 4, no. 7, (July–August 1879): 294–97.

5. William J. Hennessey, "The Architectural Works of Henry Van Brunt" (Ph.D. diss., Columbia University, 1979) provides a good overview of Van Brunt's career. For Van Brunt on Labrouste, see Henry Van Brunt, "Greek Lines (part 2)," *Atlantic Monthly* 7, no. 45 (July 1861): 76–88.

6. Hennessey, "The Architectural Works of Henry Van Brunt," 144.

7. Ibid., 132.

8. John Shaw Billings papers, 1862–1913, Box 84, New York Public Library. Early drawings of the buildings with his notations are among Billings's papers. See also letters received, and press copies of letters sent, pertaining to the construction of the Army Medical Museum and Library and Annex, Record of the Office of Public Buildings and Public Parks of the National Capitol 1790–1992, Record Group 42, National Archives Building, Washington, D.C.

9. Charles H. Baumann, *The Influence of Angus Snead MacDonald and the Snead Bookstack on Library Architecture* (Metuchen, NJ: Scarecrow Press, 1972).

10. John S. Billings, *The Principles of Ventilation and Heating* (New York: The Sanitary Engineer, 1884), in John Shaw Billings papers, 1862–1913, Box 46, New York Public Library.

11. For example, Ware advised on the competitions for the Passaic County Courthouse and Baltimore Courthouse.

12. John Shaw Billings records, 1885–1915, Box 34, New York Public Library; for example, Justin Winsor claimed the Boston Public Library was "planned to produce the largest instead of the smallest average distance of books from the point of delivery." See Kenneth A. Breisch, *Henry Hobson Richardson and the Small Public Library in America* (Cambridge, MA: MIT Press, 1997),: 86.

13. William H. Jordy, *American Buildings and Their Architects* (Garden City, NY: Anchor Books 1976); Mark A. Hewitt, Kate Lemos, William Morrison, and Charles D. Warren, *Carrère & Hastings, Architects* (New York: Acanthus Press, 2006).

14. John M. Carrère, "Ethics of Architectural Competitions," *Engineering* 5, no. 2 (May 1893): 144–50.

15. Ibid.

16. Thomas Hastings, *Thomas Hastings, Architect: Collected Writings Together with a Memoir,* by David Gray (Boston: Houghton Mifflin, 1933), 79–99.

17. Thomas Hastings, "High Buildings and Good Architecture, What Principles Should Govern Their Design," *The American Architect and Building News* 46, no. 986 (November 17, 1894): 67–68.

18. Ibid.

19. Thomas Hastings, "Modern Architecture," in Ralph Adams Cram, Thomas Hastings, and Claude Bragon, *Six Lectures on Architecture* (Chicago: University of Chicago Press, 1917).

JOHN WENRICH

INTO THE LOOKING GLASS
NEW YORK'S SKYSCRAPERS GO DOWN A RABBIT HOLE?

ALLAN GREENBERG

For it is easier, God says, to ruin than to build.
—Charles Péguy

Any casual observer of New York City can attest to the prolific skyscraper building boom unfolding in our midst. From Central Park to the Financial District, cranes raising ultra-tall towers proliferate like toadstools after a spring shower. But what architectural legacy will they leave?

Preliminary results are not encouraging. Despite the overwhelming resources—financial, artistic, aesthetic, and otherwise—at their disposal, architects, developers, and high-end consumers are driving a race to the bottom in terms of enduring design, historic significance, and contribution to the city's social and cultural fabric. Some might call me—a career-long classical architect—an outmoded critic huffing over changing times. But I am no enemy of modernism or innovation—far from it. I challenge today's dismal design trends not merely on aesthetic grounds, but because they betray New York's cultural heritage and urban integrity, often at the cost of diminishing the quality of life in the city. I wonder if in another fifty years anyone will want to celebrate the post-1960s parts of New York or lavish praise on the beauty of its new streets, parks, and buildings.

Before getting into specifics, let's ask: what constitutes good urban architecture? A beautiful city building should establish harmony not only among its own elements but also externally with its surroundings. It should elevate the mind and inspire the imagination. But most of all, good urban architecture should enhance the civic realm where many people—not only residents—observe, use, and occupy the space between and around architectural structures.

Fig. 1. Rockefeller Center by Associated Architects, 1931–38. Rendering by John Wenrich.

Urban architecture forms the fabric of the *polis.* Perhaps the best example of this in New York is Rockefeller Center, a group of fourteen Art Deco office buildings planned and designed by Associated Architects and constructed between 1930 and 1938 (fig. 1). Its four similar five-story buildings on Fifth Avenue occupy two city blocks. The pair to the north frame St. Patrick's Cathedral and connect to a tall office building. The pair to the south presents a gently scaled, invitingly symmetrical front to Fifth Avenue, framing a pedestrian shopping street,

Any new skyscraper, wishfully or not, interacts with the city's chorus of existing ones.

the Promenade—which links the Saks Fifth Avenue store, across Fifth Avenue, to an extraordinary sunken plaza that is used as a skating rink in winter. The linchpin of the fourteen-building composition is the seventy-story RCA Building (now known as 30 Rockefeller Plaza), one of New York's most beautiful skyscrapers and the Center's tallest building (see fig. 19). The vertical axis of this tower aligns with the horizontal axis of the Promenade, and these serve as the spine of the Center's composition. It is the core around which the rest of the Center has grown.

No other urban space in New York even begins to approach Rockefeller Center's success. It is of the city as much as it is in it, capable of absorbing and contributing to the ambience of New York and merging with the aesthetic and symbolic ideals of the United States. As Rockefeller Center illustrates, it is that unceasing dialogue between buildings and people going about their lives that distinguishes great urban architecture from art or ordinary construction. It is not just an artistic enterprise; it is a civic one.

The truth is that New York skyscrapers have a uniquely important historical identity; any new skyscraper, wishfully or not, interacts with the city's chorus of existing ones. New York's were the world's first really tall skyscrapers. They captivated the imagination as secular cathedrals, drawing inspiration from American civic structures like the Capitol and the Washington Monument, and using carved stone finishes, arched windows, gilded cupolas, and pinnacles to inspire awe (fig. 2). The 1,454-foot-high Empire State Building of 1931 (fig. 3), which in the eyes of New Yorkers will always be the tallest and most beautiful skyscraper of all, is the very symbol of our great city. It is anthropomorphic; it uses its multiple setbacks and pyramidal massing to access our innate sense of gravity and our body's sense of its own stability. And by gathering up around itself all the skyscrapers in the city, the Empire State Building seems to dominate the skyline. Its design accounts for the building's status as a movie icon—it has featured in more than 250 films, including the 1993 classic *Sleepless in Seattle*. Where else but on The Empire State's Observation Deck could Meg Ryan, coming from Baltimore, and Tom Hanks from Seattle with his eight-year-old son meet on a blind date?

Looking at New York skyscrapers built in the 1920s and '30s, one is struck by the sheer number of impressive skyscrapers and the picturesque splendor of both the skyline and the streetscape. These buildings were bold, noble, assertive, steel-framed and masonry-clad homages to New York's ideals of market capitalism, freedom, opportunity, and human accomplishment. They use the skyscraper form to emphasize height, sculptural beauty,

Fig. 2. Details of the top of the Consolidated Edison Building (originally Consolidated Gas Co.) by Warren & Wetmore, 1927.

solidity, and human scale. But, perhaps most important of all, they add to the ambience of the sidewalk by virtue of their imaginatively detailed shop fronts, solid construction, and tiered form (fig. 4).

Many of these characteristics are directly traceable to the New York City Building Zone Resolution of 1916. This first attempt to regulate tall buildings was adopted after the looming bulk of the thirty-six-story Equitable Building (1915) provoked a sense of crisis and sharpened the desire to avoid transforming the entire city into a network of dark streets. It was a brilliantly successful law that was rationally based on a defined angle projected from the opposite side of the street to limit a building's mass at certain heights. The law improved the quality of light and the sense of openness on the sidewalks as well as inside adjacent offices. No height limit was set, but gross building area was limited to a percentage of lot size. In 1922, the delineator Hugh Ferriss made renderings of possible architectural forms and maximum building volumes resulting from the new zoning (fig. 5). When these were later collected in *The Metropolis of Tomorrow* (1929), they provided a foretaste of the city's greatest period of skyscraper design.

Innovations in steel framing and curtain wall construction enabled the transformation of the lower Manhattan skyline. Since the 1890s, it has captivated the world's imagination as one building after another reached skyward: the Park Row Building of 1899 was overtopped by the Singer Building in 1908, and that was exceeded in height by the Woolworth Building in 1913. The same intense level of aesthetic ingenuity in midtown gave rise to the Chrysler Building in 1930, RCA Building in 1933, and the Empire State Building in 1931. By 1932, when the sixty-seven-story Cities Services Building was constructed, the skyline and skyscrapers of lower Manhattan represented the "metropolis of tomorrow" (fig. 6).

Photo: Museum of the City of New York

Fig. 3. Empire State Building by Shreve, Lamb & Harmon, 1931.

Photo: Ed Westmacott/Alamy Stock Photo

Fig. 4. Sidewalk view of the Fred F. French Building (551 Fifth Avenue) by H. Douglas Ives and John Sloane, 1927.

Photo: Avery Architectural & Fine Arts Library, Columbia University, by permission of the artist's family

Fig. 5. *Night in the Science Zone* from *The Metropolis of Tomorrow*, drawing by Hugh Ferriss, 1929.

Fig. 6. Lower Manhattan skyline before 1950.

The typical New York skyscraper was divided into three parts. The first was a base, at street level, usually three to five stories, frequently lined by beautifully designed storefronts. Often, the base was distinguished from the rest of the building by different window sizes, as occured at the Chrysler Building (fig. 7); on other buildings, there may have been a setback, a change of materials, or a shift in the sculptural character of the massing. The second was a middle, usually distinguished in design from the base. It was essentially a multistory shaft, more austere, and often dynamically sculpted by means of setbacks and vertical indentations. Last, there was a multistory crown at the top, formed by domes, spires, pyramids, and other fantastic forms to advertise New York to everyone approaching from distant horizons. Architects' imaginations could run wild on these forms. These skyscrapers were conceived as three-dimensional structures with distinctive silhouettes and were carefully related to their place in the city.

After World War II, some new buildings continued to develop this complex urbanism using setbacks, continuous horizontal bands of windows, and more radical new aesthetic directions, as we see on the exquisite, south-facing, side street facade of 979 Third Avenue, the D & D building (1963), by Emery Roth & Sons (fig. 11).

In the 1950s, however, a new and different generation of skyscrapers emerged, still using frame construction and curtain walls, but now with rectangular building masses and an independent skin of glass unrelated to the building's interior. Unlike the older prewar skyscrapers, these new versions were often designed without setbacks or any consideration of the character of surrounding buildings and neighborhoods.

The first such building to consciously violate the integrity of its setting was Lever House (1952) on Park Avenue (fig. 8). Although it was erected on a serene boulevard lined with continuous masonry facades,

this glass-walled building was freestanding. Designed by Gordon Bunshaft of Skidmore, Owings & Merrill (SOM), Lever House thwarts its context and juxtaposes two weightless, counterbalanced, rectangular masses. One is a twenty-one-story slab along East Fifty-fourth Street; the other is a single-story-high horizontal podium floating over the entire site. Beneath the podium is an open plaza, but at the plaza's center, just where it should be darkest, Bunshaft cut out a large opening in the podium mass above, creating a light-filled public park. Then, with uncharacteristic wit, he planted a tree-lined garden on the roof, rather than on the plaza itself—an homage to Le Corbusier.

This is all done with great panache, and the novelty of the design gave license to glory in the revolt against any convention or guideline. Ezra Pound's often misunderstood motto "Make it new!" was enlisted in service of the modernist revolt. The Lever House design, however,

exposed the blank side walls of the adjacent structures, and it decisively interrupted the continuous facade of the buildings lining Park Avenue. By ignoring this context and the neighboring Racquet & Tennis Club (1918) by McKim, Mead & White, Bunshaft portrayed prewar New York as obsolete and proposed Lever House as the exemplary model for a new avant-garde city of freestanding buildings. I don't believe any other American architect of that time could have made as potent and eloquent an anti-urban architectural statement.

The single and brightest beacon in the post–World War II cosmos of skyscrapers in New York remains Mies van der Rohe's Seagram Building (fig. 9). Completed in 1958, this masterpiece is truly the only worthy successor to the city's earlier skyscraper architecture. Following prewar tradition, the building has a base, middle, and top. Its austere, but noble plaza and subtly modeled bronze facade engage in an intense conversation with the simi-

Photo: Prints and Photographs Division, Library of Congress, Washington, D.C.

Fig. 7. Chrysler Building by William Van Allen, 1929.

Photo: © Ezra Stoller/ESTO

Fig. 8. Lever House by Skidmore, Owings & Merrill (SOM), 1952.

Photo: Ed Howard

Fig. 9. Seagram Building by Mies van der Rohe, 1958, showing the luminous ceiling from the street.

Fig. 10. One Chase Manhattan Plaza (128 Liberty St.), center, by Skidmore, Owings & Merrill (SOM), 1961.

Fig. 11. D & D Building (979 Third Avenue) by Emery Roth & Sons, 1963. View from 58th Street.

Fig. 12. Colgate-Palmolive Building (300 Park Avenue) by Emery Roth & Sons, 1954.

Fig. 13. Manufacturers Trust Company Building (510 Fifth Avenue) by Skidmore, Owings & Merrill (SOM), 1954.

Fig. 14. Downtown Manhattan skyline c. 2000, showing the World Trade Center.

larly symmetrical Racquet & Tennis Club across Park Avenue. Mies was trained as a stonemason and lacked formal education in architecture. This, along with his early experience designing classical buildings, sets him apart as what I call a "classical modernist."

The critical feature at Seagram is the remarkable luminous ceiling. Similar on every floor, its grid aligns with the vertical divisions of the building's exterior window wall and its module of structure. For an observer looking up at the building, these interrelated grids transform its mass into a unique, cohesive, and modulated three-dimensional volume. This expression of building volume stands as a polar contrast to most tall, modern buildings, which treat glass curtain wall facades as independent of their structure, ceiling, lighting, and interior spaces. In the majority of modern skyscrapers, the glass curtain walls envelop the building's mass like wrapping paper, producing a sense of chaos when viewed from the sidewalk.

Over the remainder of the 1950s, Skidmore, Owings & Merrill extended its intellectual and architectural dominance of New York and American architecture with the jewel-like Manufacturers Trust Company of 1954 (fig. 13), and other midtown buildings. Yet, in the same year, the Colgate-Palmolive Building (fig. 12) at 300 Park Avenue,

by Emery Roth & Sons, revealed limits to these modernist ideals. This building's static, rectangular masses were wrapped in dull glass curtain walls and covered almost the entire site. Although it was well built, it initiated the ruination of the urban character of New York.

This was consummated downtown in 1961 by Bunshaft's sixty-story One Chase Manhattan Plaza (fig. 10). Critic Carter B. Horsley has noted that "this huge, shiny, boxy skyscraper ruined the lower Manhattan skyline that had been, up until its erection, the most romantic and famous in the world because of its spindly tall towers that rose almost symmetrically in its center." The Twin Towers (1973), designed by Minoru Yamasaki, together with Emery Roth & Sons, delivered the coup-de-grâce to lower Manhattan. This pair of identical towers constantly drew attention to itself, undermining the scale and coherence of the skyline (fig. 14). The deluge of tall, boring, and illiterate glass buildings with large floor plates that followed transformed lower Manhattan from the soaring city of skyscrapers into the squat city of boring buildings.

So how do we account for, on the one hand, the architectural and engineering feats that produced the great pre-1950 skyscrapers and skyline of Manhattan, and

Photo: © Anne Day

Fig. 15. 432 Park Avenue by Rafael Viñoly Architect, 2017.

Photo: Wade Zimmerman

Fig. 16. One57 (157 W. 57th Street) by Christian de Portzamparc, 2011.

on the other, the recent decline in quality of architecture and urbanism or the unfulfilled promise of a skyscraper like Seagram? Building beautiful skyscrapers, which enhance our great city, has never had anything to do with repeating the past, or eschewing structural or other engineering innovations, as some modernists assert. Surely there are other causes.

One cause can be found in the 1961 revision of the 1916 Building Zone Resolution, which embedded the anti-urban impulses of Lever House in law. It also allowed and even encouraged the design of box-like buildings with plazas in front instead of consistent, street-defining facades with tiered setbacks above them. Ironically, this change in the code was, to a degree, inspired by Seagram. Sadly, in less able hands than Mies's, these plazas proved ruinous.

Unlike the 1916 resolution, which created the particular and distinct beauty of skyscraper and skyline in both lower and midtown Manhattan, the result of the 1961 law was incoherent city planning. Proof of the weakness of the urbanism and architecture it engendered can be seen readily in those parts of the city where very few older buildings remain. They tend to look as bleak as

The building at 432 Park Avenue is 1,396 feet tall. Designed by Rafael Viñoly, it is taller than One World Trade Center without its visually disconnected mast (fig. 15). The austere design of this assertive, self-referential, obelisk-like form is an inescapable feature of the skyline, but from the sidewalk of Park Avenue it is a surprisingly shy composition. The tower is partially hidden behind Viñoly's lower five-story wing along Park Avenue known as the retail cube. This arrangement mitigates the overwhelming impact 432 would have if it rose directly from the sidewalk.

The building's main entrance is on East Fifty-sixth Street. But it may be approached by way of a bland tunnel through the retail cube that connects Park Avenue to a small park planted with a grid of birch trees and the edge of the tower's south facade. Alas, this wonderful idea of a "propylaea," to articulate the Park Avenue entrance and shield the street from the tower, remains unexploited. But the weakest link in the design is the main entrance itself where the sills of the 10 by 10 foot window grid, which covers the entire facade, sit directly on the ground causing the first floor to appear squeezed by the weight of the building above. This circumstance is made worse by the entrance itself, two sets of paired glass doors bisected by the solid mid-line of the building's grid.

Although One57 by Christian de Portzamparc shares a vision of the skyscraper as a simplified form, it is more experimental in its use of colored glass and in its massing. Portzamparc refers to the shimmering character of the multiple colors of glass, which animates the east and west facades as the "Klimt effect," a reference to Gustav Klimt's use of variously colored rectangular divisions, which can be seen in portraits of Adele Bloch-Bauer.

The mass of this seventy-five-floor building is asymmetrical and the four sides are subtly modulated by setbacks, each topped with a quarter circle of glass to suggest an abutment and a unified mass (fig. 16). The setbacks on West Fifty-seventh Street rise to different heights related to the adjacent buildings, and the serpentine panels of glass just below them "undulate" down the facade, "morphing" into dramatic canopies over the entrances. But these daring panels are an arbitrary imposition on the design, and at the sidewalk this building lacks any real recognition of the public realm.

One of the most remarkable new buildings is 56 Leonard Street, by Herzog & de Meuron, a sixty-story apartment building that changes plan on each of its upper floors (fig. 17). The building has a distinctive silhouette,

Fig. 17. 56 Leonard Street by Herzog & de Meuron, 2017.

the new parts of Shanghai, London, or of any American city, whether it is Dallas, Los Angeles, or Chicago. An extreme expression of the fluidity of development rights transferred between adjacent parcels made possible by the zoning changes in 1961 and after is the very tall, spindly, residential tower rising from a small footprint. Many examples are in construction just south of Central Park or in Tribeca and their thin profiles already stand out against the city's lower and fuller buildings. Three of the most interesting of these are 432 Park Avenue, One57 on West Fifty-seventh Street, and 56 Leonard Street.

and from a distance it appears that the number of balconies decreases and the height of the apartments increases as the building rises. This imbues the mass with an extraordinary lightness, almost weightlessness, as if it is stretching to touch the sky.

Although these three buildings add considerable interest to the city's inventory of new architecture, they add little to its urban qualities. This is because there is no recognition of context and, with the exception of 432 Park Avenue, no effort to enhance the experience of pedestrians. It is difficult, if not impossible to achieve real urbanism given their architects' rejection of the idea of differentiating between base, middle, and top.

Because modernism, unlike every form of architecture that came before it, has never been able to create good background buildings, the "new" city, built since 1950, is characterized by bland, often mediocre architecture, most of which adds ever more incoherence to the urban experience. We have to wonder if it is the destiny of our once great city to be transformed into a huge international shopping mall and office park.

Two recent buildings may suggest one possible way to improve the architectural character of new construction in New York through the idea of contextualism. This idea proposes that in cities, new buildings should harmonize with older, adjacent ones. Thus Cesar Pelli's 731 Lexington Avenue (2005) is unusual because it is so carefully related to the height of the surrounding buildings and it also provides an elliptical public plaza in the center of the full-block building mass (fig. 18). In

Fig. 18. 731 Lexington Avenue by Pelli, Clarke, Pelli Architects, 2005.

Photo: © Jeff Goldberg/ESTO

another example, Robert A.M. Stern uses multiple small setbacks to effectively articulate the mass of his building at 30 Park Place (see Professional Portfolio, p. 69) in a more traditional way. But the base of this building is unrelated to its middle and fails to enhance the sidewalk. Neither of these buildings provide a visually interesting top or striking fenestration. So, one has to ask if this contextualism on its own is enough.

The 1916 Building Zone Resolution was both a legal document and a new vision for the architectural character of the city. Today, zoning and other controls on development are legal documents lacking any architectural vision to similarly shape the city. In fact, the planning tradition that created the beautiful cities and towns of ancient Greece and Rome, and then of Europe and the United States, has been completely lost and the modernistic city planning that replaced it has been discredited by urban renewal and other failures. City planning is now the province of lawyers and developers whose interests usually center solely on profit, leaving the public realm unrepresented and adrift.

Just compare Rockefeller Center to the new complex of buildings now rising to replace the destroyed World Trade Center. The former still remains fresh, relevant, and innovative despite the passage of eight decades; the latter is merely another complex of unrelated office buildings grouped around the 9/11 Memorial. Urban vitality was achieved by classical and Art Deco architects with such ease, but now it seems beyond reach.

I believe that modernistic architects have failed New York. Lever House may be the one truly modern building in that it proposes a new way to build in cities. But, one has to ask, how much of what has been called modern since then similarly rethinks architecture and urbanism; and to what extent has recent modern architecture devolved into an echo chamber that blasts other approaches to architecture? By ignoring existing urbanism or demolishing older classical or Gothic-style buildings, proponents of this close-minded version of modern architecture refuse any discussion of alternative approaches to architecture—even silencing debate in the architectural press and at many of our great universities.

In his 2008 study *Modernism, the Lure of Heresy*, historian Peter Gay reminds us the two important generators of modernism were "the lure of heresy" and a "yearning for absolute artistic autonomy." A genius like Picasso or Le Corbusier may have succeeded with this approach, but to believe we lesser mortals are capable of the same genius is a fallacy. As we have seen, Lever House undermined conventions to express just such untrammeled artistic authority, with some success. But the banality of so many modernistic buildings makes one question whether it leaves any real hope for a genuine urbanism if all architects do the same.

New York is a city under siege—it is threatened by modernistic architecture and urbanism. The same forces are also in the process of decimating the beautiful skyline of the City of London where once the great dome of St. Paul's Cathedral and its flock of fifty-five neighborhood church steeples were instantly recognizable and justly admired. Now, this glorious skyline has been replaced by a crude agglomeration of characterless office buildings, similar to buildings in dozens of modern cities. And in Paris, citizens are waging a valiant battle against architects and politicians who wish to allow skyscrapers to be built in the City of Light. This does not auger well for the future of New York or any of the world's great and ancient cities.

Finally, any modern-trained architect trying to learn how to design a classical building can tell you it is easier to destroy something beautiful than to equal the wonderful buildings of the past with something built from scratch. Lacking a vision of urbanism, most of today's architects prefer to present their buildings as isolated events rather than as a part of a greater whole. The quest for absolute architectural control precludes any recognition of the public realm, as it seeks to avoid comparison with the architecture of the Empire State Building and the urbanism of Rockefeller Center. By recognizing the successes of the past and keeping open minds for the future, we can do better.

Photo: Gottscho-Schleisner, Inc. Prints and Photographs Division, Library of Congress, Washington, D.C.

Fig. 19. The RCA Building during the construction of Rockefeller Center.

Allan Greenberg was born in South Africa and educated at the University of Witwatersrand and Yale University. He became a U. S. citizen in 1973 and established his architecture firm, which has offices in New York City and Alexandria, Virginia. His completed projects are found throughout the United States. Monographs of his work were published in 1995 and 2013. His most recent books include *The Architecture of Democracy: American Architecture and the Legacy of the Revolution*, and *Lutyens and the Modern Movement*.

THE EXTRAORDINARY CITY OF AGONISTS

STEPHEN ALESCH AND ROBIN STANDEFER

Early in its history, New York City decided it would be a city of contrasts and opposites and this is why we choose to work and play here. It is a city made of cheese and chalk, of compositional and structural opposites, completely and totally unresolved. A city where order and disorder bark and honk in a constant noisy chase. A city with a penchant for 7:00 a.m. jackhammers and mysterious afternoon silence on job sites. This is a city that left out alleys so trash is piled high at the curb and angry trash men are there every morning to greet you, grinding and belching at dawn's early light. Yet the same disorderly city just recently slid the 150-year-old Washington Square fountain twenty-three feet across the park to align it with the George Washington Arch and Fifth Avenue—just because things needed to be tidied up a bit. From its pell-mell cow path downtown to its unrelenting 1811 grid, it spreads up and then spills over to its low-rise boroughs. New York—the Center of Agonism!

The city has never been able to find a normal middle ground, nor has anyone in it. The lonely upward sprawl of the glassy reflections of its modernist boxes compete with its beautiful brownstones, its Beaux-Arts bombshells, its woop woop starchitecture, and its massive, picturesque park (where curvilinear asymmetry and thuggy squirrels rule). It is a city where the Metropolitan Museum of Art presents its beautiful, careful facade and formal stage-like stair, but once inside we find 150 years of clashing, accumulated circulation unfolding before us like an unresolved argument. The range of archi-

tectural expression in New York is immense, and the range of the emotion it generates is wide—graceful and not, careful and not, thoughtful and not. It's a mix that somehow works and is neither too neat nor too sloppy. Its ratio of order to disorder, of thorns to soft leaves, is a ratio that may be just quite right for a city.

New York is essentially a self-centered city. It is impossible find its spiritual or geometric center, so you, and that spot you happen to be standing upon, are its center. Denied a backyard to hide in and inhabiting relatively small office spaces and apartments, New York's citizens revel in misbehaving, showing off in public spaces, and entertaining tour-

In New York you are part of the story of conflict, of compression and expansion . . .

ists. When architects create public spaces—stages and environments where these capricious acts occur—they are simply doing the same thing: misbehaving, showing off, and entertaining tourists—albeit with their projects. One could say the combustion engine of the city is the activity in these restaurants and bars we create. These are the places where explosive acts and deals turn the city's crankshaft. These New York moments are impossible to capture, as one can never step back far enough to properly frame the shot. Clearly, we are all in the shot and we cannot get out of it because these streets are too narrow in one direction and endless in the other. In New York, you are part of this story of conflict, of compression and expansion whether you like it or not.

Fig. 1. *Center for Humanity.* Proposal for the World Trade Center site by Stephen Alesch of Roman and Williams, 2002.

In this city, we are "never astray, yet are always lost," as Jean-Paul Sartre said in 1945, but then again the French are not known for their sense of humor. For if it wasn't humor, what was it that allowed a street like Broadway to keep its odd broken angles despite the city planners' rigid grid? It is a street laid out as if it were a walk through a field of flowers. Somehow, while the city's planners plowed down farms, homes, and hills and filled rivers to install their ironclad grid, Broadway remained untouched, creating a thousand accidents, happy and unhappy, where the two ideas tangle. There are probably many origin myths about why Broadway's path was kept. Our version is simple: It is an allegory for this city's love of order and its fascination with disorder, its untamable, playful nature and simultaneously, its deadly serious spirit. The surveyor's team let it be; perhaps one of them was fired, another given a medal. Agonists. Beautiful.

This is why we live and work here and this is why we will one day move away to the sea and rest—soon, we hope, because it is an absolutely exhausting and crazy place. It is not utopian, it is not beautiful, but we are not looking for beauty when, say, we go to meet someone of great character, a great thinker, or great agonist. It will be a joy to look from another time and place upon the small mark we made to a handful of the city's 700,000 nearly identical but totally unique plots. If you happen to get your hands on one of these lots, we hope you put up something careful and disciplined, and we also hope some part of it is unfinished, untamed, and maybe even confusing—to reflect the wild spirit of New York.

Fig. 2. *The Order and Disorder of Daily Life in New York City.* Drawing by Stephen Alesch of Roman and Williams, 2017.

Robin Standefer studied at the Art Students League and the Academia di Belle Arti di Firenze. She attended Smith College and graduated from Hampshire College with a Liberal Arts degree.

Stephen Alesch attended Northern Arizona University. He left the university for an architectural apprenticeship, and for ten years, worked for the firms of Quentin Dart Parker and Venice Atelier.

The two met in the 1990s while working in Hollywood as production designers and art directors. Together, they designed more than twenty Hollywood films. In 2002, they opened their own firm, Roman and Williams Buildings and Interiors, where they design houses, apartment buildings, restaurants, hotels, and furniture. Standefer and Alesch are married and live in New York City.

PROFESSIONAL
PORTFOLIO

GRAND CENTRAL
TERMINAL

Additional images of work in the Professional Portfolio
can be found at classicist.org/portfolios

151 East 78th Street, Manhattan
Peter Pennoyer Architects
Client: Spruce Capital Partners

Residential building with 14 condominium apartments.
New construction. Reinforced concrete with brick and Indiana limestone facades;
17 stories, 170 feet tall, 66,000 square feet.

135 East 79th Street, Manhattan
Studio Sofield   Architect of Record: SLCE Architects
Client: The Brodsky Organization

Photo: Studio Sofield

Residential building with 32 condominium apartments.
New construction. Carved stone, custom hand-laid brick, and ironwork;
19 stories, 210 feet tall, 144,239 square feet.

Carhart Mansion, 3 East 95th Street, Manhattan
Zivkovic Connolly Architects PC and John Simpson & Partners LTD
Residential building with four apartments. New construction. Indiana limestone; 7 stories, 75 feet tall, 50,000 square feet.

Photos: © Peter Aaron / OTTO

30 Park Place, Manhattan
Robert A.M. Stern Architects   Architect of Record: SLCE Architects
Client: Silverstein Properties
Four Seasons Hotel with 189 rooms and 157 condominium apartments. New construction. Indiana limestone
and precast concrete clad tower; 82 stories, 926 feet tall, 717,075 square feet.

Photo: Fairfax and Sammons

345–353 State Street, Brooklyn
Fairfax & Sammons Architecture   Architect of Record: Steven F. Levine Architects
Client: IBEC and Strategic Development Corporation
Row of seven 15-foot-wide townhouses (three single-family units and four with two units each). New construction.
Brick on block with cast iron-stone trim and a sheet-metal cornice; 5 stories, 25,200 square feet.

Photo: Francis Dzikowski

2, 2A, 4 Strong Place, Cobble Hill, Brooklyn
CWB Architects
Client: Brennan Real Estate, LLC
Three four-story townhouse units and a two-story carriage house. New construction.
Brick, brownstone trim, and painted ironwork; each townhouse 3,900 square feet.

Photo: Lisa Romerein

Park Avenue Apartment, Manhattan
Ferguson and Shamamian Architects

Photo: Durston Saylor

Central Park South Apartment, Manhattan
John B. Murray Architect

Photo: Durston Saylor

Park Avenue Apartment, Manhattan
John B. Murray Architect

Photo: Wade Zimmerman

Private Club, Manhattan
Allan Greenberg Architect

Photo: Eric Piasecki

Fifth Avenue Apartment, Manhattan
G.P. Schafer Architect, PLLC

Photo: Tara Fedoriw-Morris

211 Elizabeth Street, Manhattan
Roman and Williams   Architect of Record: Michael Muroff Architect
Client: Dune Capitol
Commercial and residential building with 17 apartments. New construction.
Handcrafted red brick and black wood; 7 stories, 35, 211 square feet.

Photo: Field Condition

The Sterling Mason Building, 71 Laight Street, Manhattan
Morris Adjmi Architects
Client: Taconic Investment Partners
Loft warehouse from 1905, now a residential building with 37 apartments. New construction and renovation. Original facade of red brick masonry, new "twin" addition with metallic aluminum facade; 7 stories, 115,000 square feet.

Photo: Donna Dotan Photography

Walker Hotel Greenwich Village, 52 West 13th Street, Manhattan
Atelier & Co.   Architect of Record: Gene Kaufmann PC
Client: Gemini Real Estate Advisors
Boutique hotel with 113 guest rooms. Exterior redesign. Brick and cast-stone trim and ornaments, copper-clad
and restoration-glass windows, gas lanterns, and a custom triglyph frieze; 18 stories, 32,500 square feet.

Photo: Eric Laignel

The Beekman, 123 Nassau Street, Manhattan
Gerner Kronick + Valcarcel, Architects   Original Architect: Benjamin Silliman, Jr. and James M. Farnsworth
Hotel with 287 rooms. Restoration; original construction completed in 1883. Philadelphia red brick, terra-cotta,
tan Dorchester Stone, Deer Isle granite, and decorative cast iron; 10 stories, approximately 130,000 square feet.

North Hall and Library, Bronx Community College, The Bronx
Robert A.M. Stern Architects   Architect of Record: Ismael Leyva Architect
Library/classroom building with double-height information commons. New construction. Clad in four-color buff-blend Roman brick with cast stone trim on precast concrete panels and standing seam zinc roof with pre-patinated copper trim; 98,600 square feet.

D & D Building Annex, 979 Third Avenue, Manhattan
Allan Greenberg Architect, LLC
Client: Cohen Brothers Realty Corp.
Commercial retail building. New construction. Glass fiber-reinforced concrete; 5 stories, 50,000 square feet.

Le Coucou, 138 Lafayette Street, Manhattan
Roman and Williams
Client: Starr Restaurants
Restaurant with 80 seats. New construction. Whitewashed in plaster and paint,
triple-hung glass windows, and exposed concrete; 32,000 square feet.

Augustine, 5 Beekman Street, Manhattan
Architect of Record: Richard H. Lewis
Keith McNally and Ian McPheely
Restaurant in the Beekman Hotel with 90 seats and bar with 17 seats. Complete renovation.
Painted burlap ceiling, custom painted earthenware tile walls, mosaic tile floor, and mahogany front and back bar;
4,205 square feet (2,147-square-foot dining room, 374-square-foot service kitchen, 1,684-square-foot cellar).

ACADEMIC
PORTFOLIO

Villa, Parco Del Celio; Rome, Italy; Alexander Preudhomme
3rd Year; Instructor: Professor Krupali Krusche

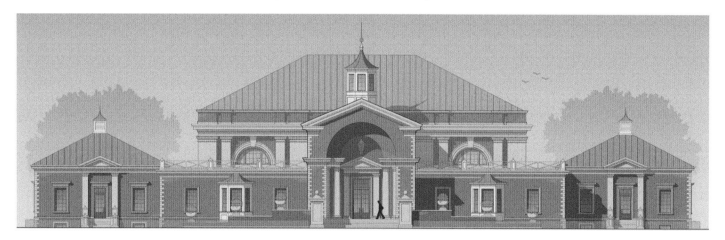

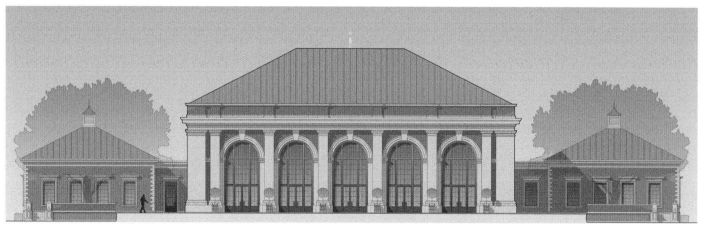

Lincoln Foundation Hall; Chicago, Illinois; Daniel Kiser
1st Year Graduate; Instructor: Professor Richard Economakis

St. Joseph County Public Library; South Bend, Indiana; Jay Hobbs
4th Year; Instructor: Professor Thomas Gordon Smith

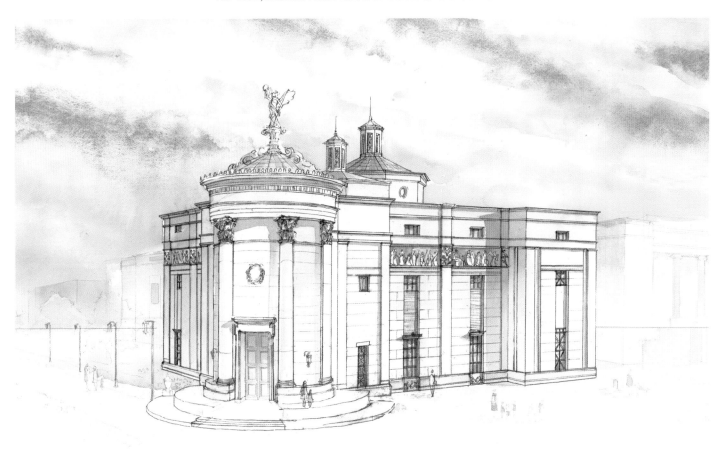

Museum of Restitutional Arts; Washington, D.C.; Margaret Zhang
4th Year; Instructor: Professor Thomas Gordon Smith

School for the Building Arts; Charleston, South Carolina; Lucas Stegeman
4th Year, Instructor: Professor Christopher Miller

St. Sophia Greek Orthodox Church; Elgin, Indiana; Michael Rabe
4th Year, Instructor: Nathaniel Brooks

UNIVERSITY OF MIAMI
Miami, Florida

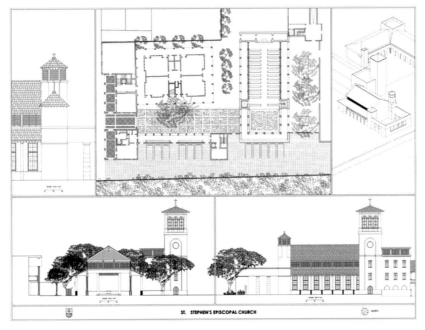

**Master Plan and Buildings for St. Stephen's Episcopal Church; Miami, Florida;
Claudia Ansorena, Hitomi Maeno, Tyler Many, and Smitha Vasan**
4th Year, 5th Year, and Graduate Studio; Instructors: Professor Frank Martinez, Visiting Critics Victoria Baran and Michael McGrattan

A Rural Schoolhouse, Daniela Déu
4th Year, Instructors: Professor Richard John, Visiting Critic Tim Kelly

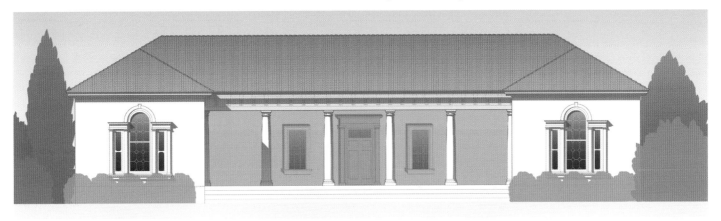

A Rural Schoolhouse, Erin Hickey
4th Year, Instructors: Professor Richard John, Visiting Critic Tim Kelly

UNIVERSITY OF COLORADO DENVER
Denver, Colorado

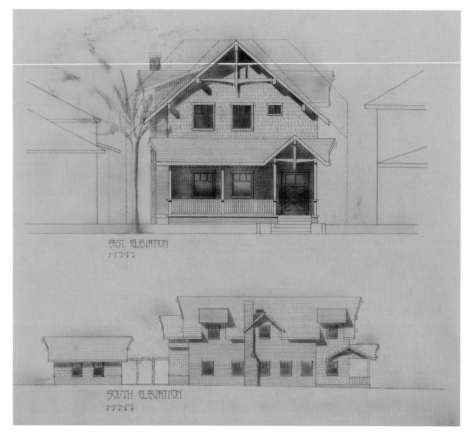

Infill Housing; Denver, Colorado; Christopher Sigit-Sidharta
Graduate Studio; Instructor: Lecturer Cameron P. Kruger

Ubuesque Theater; Denver, Colorado; Catherine Anne Crain
Graduate Studio, Instructor: Professor Laurence Keith Loftin III

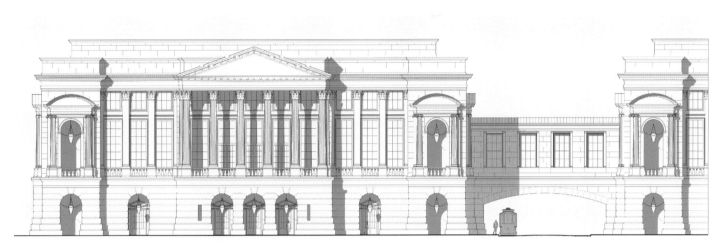

Columbus Circle Opera House; Washington D.C.; Chas Winebrenner
4th Year, Instructor: Professor James McCrery

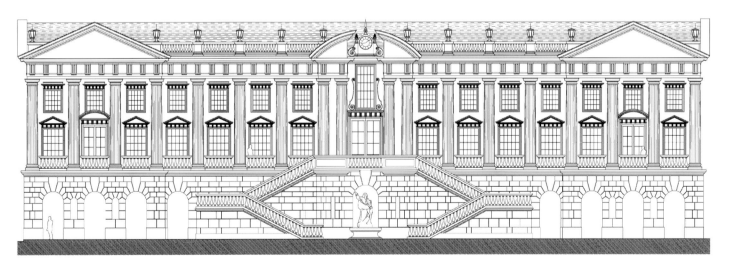

Columbus Circle Opera House; Washington D.C.; Michael Taylor
4th Year, Instructor: Professor James McCrery

New Connecticut Statehouse; New Haven, Connecticut; Stephanie Jazmines
Graduate Design Studio, Instructors: Visiting Professor Leon Krier, George Knight

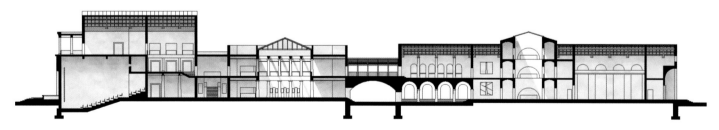

A New School and Gallery; New Haven, Connecticut; Jingwen Li
Graduate Design Studio, Instructors: Visiting Professor Leon Krier, George Knight

YALE UNIVERSITY
New Haven, Connecticut

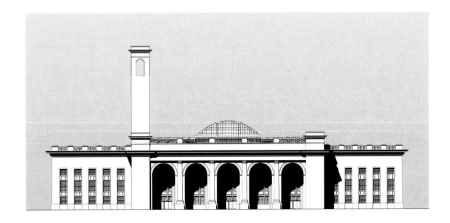

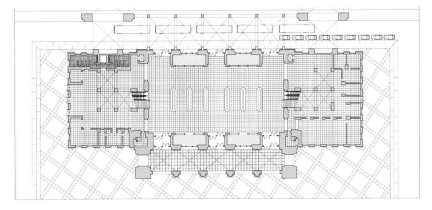

Alterations to Union Station; New Haven, Connecticut; Ian Spencer
Graduate Design Studio, Instructors: Visiting Professor Leon Krier, George Knight

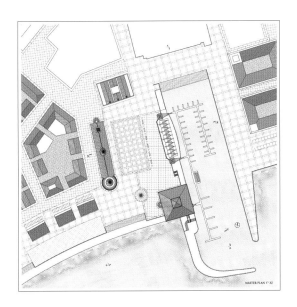

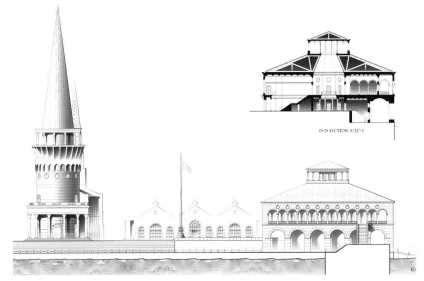

New Marina with Market, Yacht Club and Gallery; New Haven, Connecticut; Jizhou Liu
Graduate Design Studio, Instructors: Visiting Professor Leon Krier, George Knight

VIRGINIA COMMONWEALTH UNIVERSITY
Richmond, Virginia

A Celtic Temple; Scotland; Smitty Lynch
Instructor: Professor Peter Hodson

KINGSTON UNIVERSITY
Kingston, England

Addition to the Gainsborough Gallery and Print Rooms; Sudbury, Suffolk, England; Peter Folland
Level 4, Instructors: Timothy Smith, Jonathan Taylor

INSTITUTE OF CLASSICAL ARCHITECTURE & ART
New York, New York

Summer Studio in Classical Architecture

Prospect Park Gate; Hamilton Brindley; Western Kentucky University
Instructors: Michael Mesko, Stephen Chrisman

Prospect Park Gate; Noah Sannes; Georgia Institute of Technology
Instructors: Michael Mesko, Stephen Chrisman

INSTITUTE OF CLASSICAL ARCHITECTURE & ART

New York, New York

Rieger Graham Prize

Study of Urban Development Along the Route of the Solenne Possesso

Capitoline Hill   **Il Gesù**

Brendan Hart, Rieger Graham Prize Recipient 2016

American Academy in Rome

Christopher H. Browne Paris Drawing Tour

The Bibliothèque Sainte-Geneviève, Leslie-Jon Vickory
Instructors: Kahlil Hamady, Andrew Zega, Bernd Dams

The Louvre, Mark Jackson
Instructors: Kahlil Hamady, Andrew Zega, Bernd Dams

Christopher H. Browne Rome Drawing Tour

The Arch of Constantine, Elena Belova
Instructors: Ben Bolgar, Richard Piccolo,
Thomas Rajkovich

The Pantheon, Martin Burns
Instructors: Ben Bolgar, Richard Piccolo,
Thomas Rajkovich

INSTITUTE OF CLASSICAL ARCHITECTURE & ART

New York, New York

Alma Schapiro Prize

Santa Maria Maggiore, ink and wash on toned paper

Copy of Antonio Gherardi's
Assumption of Mary, oil on linen

**Bernini's Nile from the Fontana dei Quattro
Fiumi, chalk on paper**

Anthony Baus, Alma Schapiro Prize Recipient 2015
American Academy in Rome

GRAND CENTRAL ATELIER
Long Island City, New York

Soldiers' and Sailors' Monument, New York; Deborah Rodriguez
Instructor: Anthony Baus

ACADEMY OF CLASSICAL DESIGN
Southern Pines, North Carolina

Laocoon Torso, charcoal and chalk on paper, Brett Downey
Instructor: Jeffrey Mims

Belvedere Torso, oil on canvas, Rodney Wilkinson
Instructor: Jeffrey Mims

Strapwork Plaster Ceiling; Charleston, South Carolina; Maggie Jo Adkins
Jr. Level; Instructor: Adjunct Professor Michael Lauer

Iron Railing with Bronze Collar; Charleston, South Carolina; Annie Arthur
Sr. Level; Instructor: Professor Frank Verga

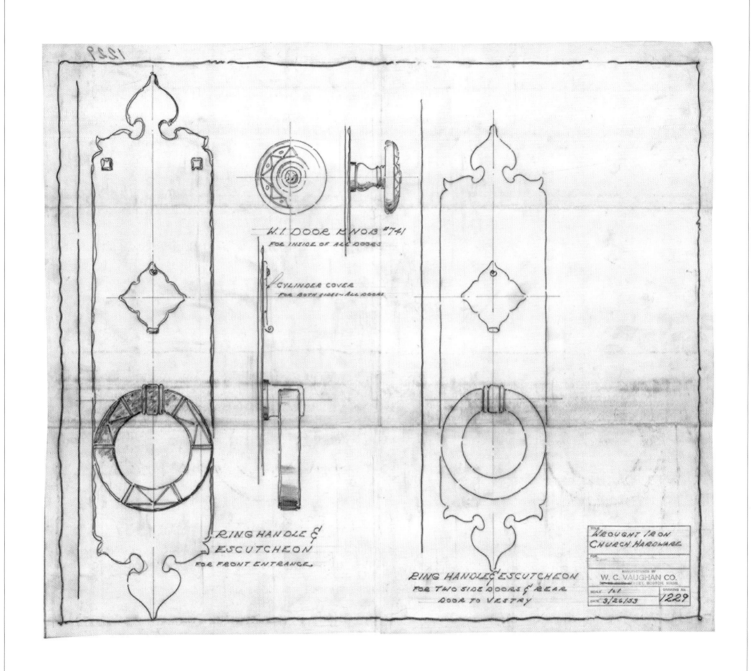

"WROUGHT IRON CHURCH HARDWARE"

Drawing No. 1229, for First Parish Church in Taunton, Massachusetts

W.C. Vaughan Co., 1953

TREMONT TEMPLE

William Washburn (Restoration)

BOSTON, MA

Restoration, 1853

THE OLD SOUTH MEETING HOUSE

BOSTON, MA

Restoration, 1857

ST. PHILIP'S EPISCOPAL CHURCH

CHARLESTON, SC

Restoration, 1927–1938

CHURCH OF THE HEAVENLY REST

Mayers, Murray & Phillip, Architects

Ostrander & Eshleman, Distributor

NEW YORK, NY

1929

MEMORIAL CHURCH OF HARVARD UNIVERSITY*

Coolidge, Shepley, Bulfinch & Abbott, Architects

CAMBRIDGE, MA

1932

ALL SAINTS CHURCH

Frohman, Robb, and Little, Architects

G. Adolph Johnson (Addition)

WORCESTER, MA

1934, 1956

NEW OLD SOUTH CHURCH

Charles Amos Cummings & William Thomas Sears, Architects

Francis Richmond Allen & Charles Collins (Addition), 1935

BOSTON, MA

1935–1937

CORPUS CHRISTI CHURCH*

Wilfred Edwards Anthony, Architect

NEW YORK, NY

1936

GRACE CHURCH

James Renwick, Jr.: Renwick, Aspinwall & Russell , Architects

NEW YORK, NY

Restoration, ca. 1937

SAINT MARY'S EPISCOPAL CHURCH*

James Renwick, Jr.: Renwick, Aspinwall & Russell, Architects

WASHINGTON, DC

Restoration, ca. 1937

WATERTOWN FIRST PARISH CHURCH

WATERTOWN, MA

Restoration, ca. 1937

CHRIST CHURCH CRANBROOK

Bertram Grosvenor Goodhue, Architect

BLOOMFIELD, MI

Addition, 1938

ST. JOSEPHS CHURCH*

1938

TRINITY CHURCH

NEWTON, MA

Alteration, 1938

CENTENARY CHURCH

WINSTON SALEM, NC

1939

FIRST CHRISTIAN CHURCH

Gottlieb Eliel Saarinen, Architect

COLUMBUS, IN

1939–1942

SAINT ANTHONY'S CHURCH*

1939

ST. MICHAEL'S PARISH

LITCHFIELD, CT*

1939

TRINITY EVANGELICAL LUTHERAN CHURCH*

NEW YORK, NY

1939

MASSACHUSETTS GENERAL HOSPITAL CHAPEL

BOSTON, MA

1940

CHURCH OF THE REDEEMER

BROOKLINE, MA

1941

Source: E.R. Butler & Co Research Library: W.C. Vaughan Co. Archives.

* *Archival Record Incomplete.*

CRONK CHAPEL*

1946

FIRST CHURCH CHRIST SCIENTIST

WINCHESTER, MA*

1946, 1958

ST. JOSEPH

DOVER, NII

1946

OLD WYE CHURCH

William Graves Perry: Perry, Shaw, & Hepburn (Restoration)

WYE MILLS, MD

Restoration, 1947–1949

FIRST LUTHERAN CHURCH

GARDNER, MA

1948

OUR LADY OF MERCY SEMINARY

LENOX, MA

1949

ST. ANDREWS EPISCOPAL CHURCH

Nathaniel Saltonstall, Architect

WELLESLEY, MA

1949

ST. THOMAS CHURCH

HARTFORD, CT

1949

ST. JOSEPH'S CATHEDRAL*

1952

ST. MARY'S - THE MORNING STAR CHURCH

PITTSFIELD, MA

1952

1717 MEETING HOUSE

WEST BARNSTABLE, WA

Restoration, 1952–1958

FIRST PARISH CHURCH*

TAUNTON, MA

1953

CATHEDRAL CHURCH OF ST. JOHN

James E. Lowe & Sons (Restoration), 1953

WILMINGTON, DE

Restoration, 1953

ST. GEORGE'S EPISCOPAL CHURCH

Samuel Fuller, Architect

SCHENECTADY, NY

Restoration, 1953

TRINITY EPISCOPAL CHURCH

Victorine du Pont & Samuel Homsey, Architects

WILMINGTON, DE

1953

BRANDEIS UNIVERSITY CHAPELS

Eero Saarinen, Architect, Master Plan

Max Abramovitz: Harrison & Abramovitz, Architect

WALTHAM, MA

1954–1963

ST. ANDREWS CHURCH

William Graves Perry: Perry, Shaw, & Hepburn, Architects

WELLESLEY, MA

1954

ST. BRIGID'S CHURCH

Curtin & Riley, Architects

WEST HARTFORD, CT

1954

CHRIST CHURCH

Abreu & Robeson, Architects

ST. SIMONS ISLAND, GA

1955

FIRST PARISH MEETING HOUSE

COHASSET, MA

Restoration, ca. 1955

HOLY TRINITY LUTHERAN CHURCH

Robert Clemmer: Clemmer Bush Sills and Abernathy, Architects

HICKORY, NC

1955

E. R. Butler & Co.

Ecclesiastical Projects

Enoch Robinson & Henry Whitney (1826)

E. & G.W. Robinson & Co. (1827–1839)

E. Robinson & Co. (1839–1904)

G.N. Wood & Co. (1904–1914)

Wm. Hall & Co. (1843–1920)

L.S. Hall & Co. (1914–1918)

John Tein Company (1883–1939)

Ostrander & Eshleman (1921–1992)

W.C. Vaughan Co. (1902-2000)

Quincy Spindle Mfg. Co. (-1999)

(New England Lock and Hardware Co.)

&

E.R. Butler & Co. (1990)

B̈

E. R. Butler & Co.

MANUFACTURERS

WWW.ERBUTLER.COM

CATALOGUES AVAILABLE TO THE TRADE

SHOWROOMS BY APPOINTMENT ONLY

DRAWINGS: ELMER HALE PRATT · TYPOGRAPHY: JOHN PACKER

UNITED CHURCH

William Graves Perry: Perry, Shaw, & Hepburn, Architects

WALPOLE, MA

1955

WEST BARNSTABLE MEETING HOUSE

E.B. Goodell, Jr (Restoration), 1955

BARNSTABLE, MA

Restoration, 1955

WESTWOOD PARISH HALL*

1956

WYE PARISH HOUSE

WYE MILLS, MD

Restoration, 1957

FIRST LUTHERAN CHURCH

Pietro Belluschi, Architect

BOSTON, MA

1957

ADELYNROOD

BYFIELD, MA

Restoration, 1959

LINCOLN PARSONAGE

LINCOLN, MA

1959

REVERE PENTECOSTAL CHURCH

REVERE, MA

1959

CHURCH IN WINSTON SALEM

WINSTOM SALEM, NC

1960

CHURCH OF ADVENT

MEDFIELD, MA

Restoration, 1960

CHRIST CHURCH

Philip Horton Smith: St. John Smith, Smith & Sellew (Polk) (Addition), 1961

HAMILTON, MA

1961

KING'S CHAPEL HOUSE

BOSTON, MA

Restoration, 1961–1964

LUTHERAN CHURCH OF THE NEWTONS

Nathaniel Saltonstall, Architect

NEWTON, MA

1961

LUTHERAN HOME OF MOORESTOWN

MOORESTOWN, NJ

1961

PILGRAM CONGREGATIONAL CHURCH*

1961

CATHEDRAL CHURCH OF ST. PAUL

BOSTON, MA

Restoration, 1962

CATHOLIC GUILD FOR THE BLIND*

1962

EPHRATA CLOISTER

EPHRATA, PA

Restoration, 1962

FIRST PARISH CHURCH

LINCOLN, MA

1962

HOLY TRINITY EPISCOPAL CHURCH

NEW YORK, NY*

1962

SONS OF MARY

FRAMINGHAM, MA

1962

TRINITY EPISCOPAL CHURCH

Anderson, Beckwith and Haible, Architects

CONCORD, MA

1962

CENTENARY METHODIST CHURCH

RICHMOND, VA*

1963

FIRST BAPTIST CHURCH

GREENSBORO, NC

1963

HARDWARE FOR CHURCH*

Ostrander & Eshleman, Distributor

NEW YORK, NY*

1963

PRESBYTERIAN CHURCH OF THE CONVENANT

Harry Barton (Addition), 1963

GREENSBORO, NC

1963

ST. COLUMBAN PARISH

Dirsa Lampron, Architect

ARLINGTON, VT

1963

FIRST PARISH CHURCH

SUDBURY, MA

1964

PEOPLE'S METHODIST CHURCH

BRADFORD, MA

1964

ST. STEPHEN'S CHURCH

Ostrander & Eshleman, Distributor

NEW YORK, NY*

1964

DUKE UNIVERSITY DIVINITY SCHOOL

DURHAM, NC

Alteration, 1965

FIRST METHODIST CHURCH

PEARLSBURG, VA

1965

NATIONAL SHRINE OF SAINT ELIZABETH ANN
SETON

EMMITSBURG, MD

*Restoration, ca. 1965**

ST. ANGELA MERICI CHURCH

METAIRE, LA*

1965

ST. JOHN'S CHAPEL

NEW YORK, NY*

1965

ST. PETER'S CHURCH

MANSET, MA

1965

ST. MATTHEW'S GERMAN EVANGELICAL
LUTHERAN CHURCH

CHARLESTON, SC

Restoration, 1965–1966

CRANWELL SCHOOL CHAPEL

LENOX, MA

1966

ST. RICHARD'S CHURCH*

1967

TRINITY CHURCH

BOSTON, MA

Restoration, 1967, 1971

CHURCH OF ST. ANDREW (EPISCOPAL)*

Carpenter Associates, Architect

MARBLEHEAD, MA

1971

FIRST CHURCH CONGREGATIONAL

Merton Stuart Barrows (Restoration)

BOXFORD, MA

Restoration, 1972

FIRST CHURCH DEDHAM

DEDHAM, MA

Restoration, 1975

THE HEBREW COLLEGE

Andrea Leers Browning (Expansion)

BROOKLINE, MA

Ca. 1980

CENTRAL SYNAGOGUE

Henry Fernbach, Architect

NEW YORK, NY

Restoration, 1998–2001

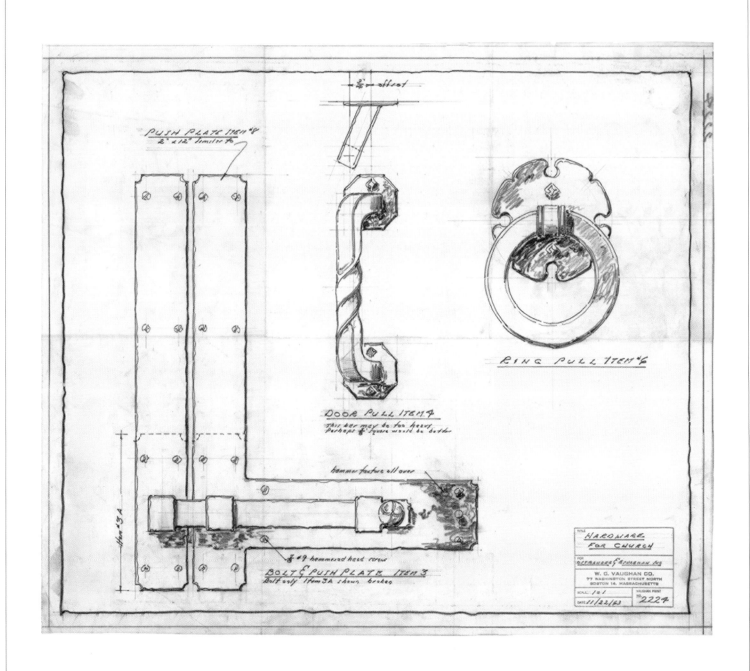

"HARDWARE FOR CHURCH"

Drawing No. 2224, for Ostrander & Eshleman

W.C. Vaughan Co., 1963

DUNCAN G. STROIK ARCHITECT, LLC

WWW.STROIK.COM

SHANGRI-LA HOTEL, PARIS

PIERRE-YVES ROCHON

PARIS | CHICAGO

THE WRIGLEY BUILDING

410 NORTH MICHIGAN AVENUE, SUITE 1600, CHICAGO, ILLINOIS 60611

TEL +1 312 980 7700 FAX +1 312 980 7710

INFO@PYR-DESIGN.COM, WWW.PYR-DESIGN.COM

ANDREW V. GIAMBERTONE

& ASSOCIATES, ARCHITECTS

GIAMBERTONEARCHITECTS.COM

JOHN B. MURRAY ARCHITECT

48 WEST 37th STREET, 10th FLOOR, NEW YORK, NY 10018

JBMARCHITECT.COM

212-242-8600

THOMAS PROCTOR ARCHITECT

LOS ANGELES, CALIFORNIA

THOMASPROCTORARCHITECT.COM

310.913.0911

MPF

MARK P. FINLAY ARCHITECTS, AIA

ARCHITECTURE & INTERIOR DESIGN

PETER PENNOYER ARCHITECTS

PPAPC.COM

A New Apartment House at 151 East 78th Street, New York City   Photography: Eric Piasecki

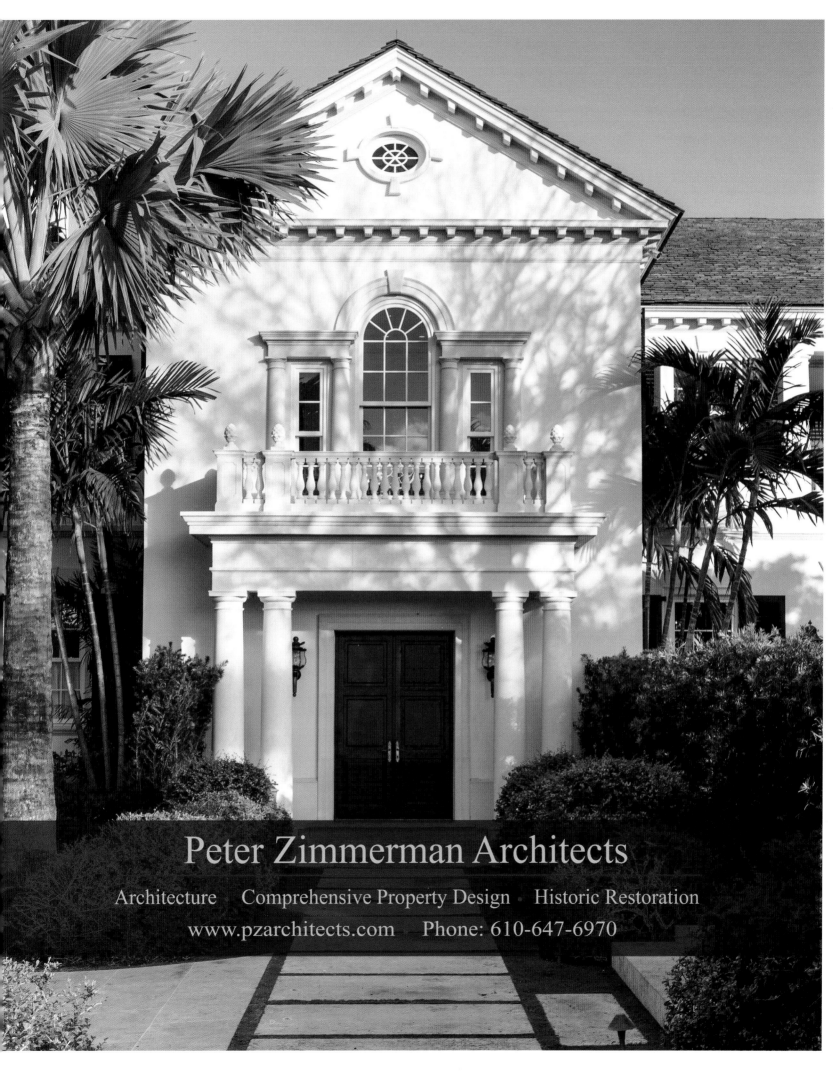

JAN GLEYSTEEN ARCHITECTS

WELLESLEY, MASSACHUSETTS
www.JanGleysteenInc.com

OLIVER COPE · ARCHITECT

135 WEST TWENTY-SIXTH STREET, NEW YORK, NEW YORK 10001

www.olivercope.com   *(212) 727-1225*

James Carpenter Design Associates Inc.
www.jcdainc.com

John Lewis Glass
www.johnlewisglass.com

Hearst Corporation, 57th & 8th St., New Yorks, Architect: Foster+Partners, © Andreas Keller

DAN GORDON
LANDSCAPE ARCHITECTS

WELLESLEY ~ EDGARTOWN
DANGORDON.COM

GREGORY LOMBARDI DESIGN

Landscape Architecture

www.LombardiDesign.com

Doyle Herman Design Associates
LANDSCAPE DESIGN

DHDA.COM

FLOWER
CONSTRUCTION

FLOWCON.NET
(908) 219-4102

SEBASTIAN
Construction Group

Building truly exceptional residences since 1948 | Dallas | Houston | www.sebastiancg.com

S.DONADIC INC

CONSTRUCTION MANAGEMENT

45-25 39TH STREET LONG ISLAND CITY NY 11104
WWW.DONADIC.COM

SOME MIGHT ONLY SEE BRICKS.

BUT WE SEE SOMETHING DIFFERENT, GRANDER, NOBLER. WE SEE SOMETHING
THE ROMANS CREATED TO BUILD THEIR WORLD. AND WE SEE THE POTENTIAL
THEY LEFT US TO BUILD YOUR VISION.

GENERAL CONTRACTOR WORKING ANYWHERE YOU NEED US.
KREKOWJENNINGS.COM, 206 625 0505

NANZAQUATIC.

CUSTOM FITTINGS MANUFACTURED TO ORDER BY THE NANZ COMPANY

118 Bay Avenue, Huntington Bay, N.Y. 11743
Phone: 631-424-0905, Fax: 631-424-4867
E-mail: info@gcmw.com
www.gcmw.com

GOLD COAST METAL WORKS
New York - Olomouc

Jamb.

Mantelpieces | Lighting | Furniture
+44 (0) 20 7730 2122 | jamb.co.uk

ARCHITECTURAL + ORNAMENTAL
METALSMITHS

LivingDesignStudios.com

aluminum · brass · bronze · copper
stainless steel · steel · wrought iron · zinc

Featuring

SUBWAY CERAMICS®
EST. 2006
A HERITAGE TILE COLLECTION

AUTHENTICITY + CRAFT
essential elements for timeless design

HERITAGETILE™
WE CARE ABOUT THE CRAFT

888.387.3280
info@heritagetile.com

Studio & Showroom
144 N. Oak Park Avenue
Oak Park, IL 60301

YOUR CLIENTS, OUR PRODUCT KNOWLEDGE

WINDOWS · DOORS · CABINETRY · MOULDING

TAGUE
DESIGN SHOWROOM
www.TagueLumber.com